Travels With George

A Memoir Through the Italy of My Childhood

OLGA VANNUCCI

Ligurian Sea Press

Copyright © 2012 Olga Vannucci

All rights reserved.

ISBN: 061562538X
ISBN-13: 978-0615625386 (Ligurian Sea Press)

DEDICATION

To my sister, Delfina.

CONTENTS

Trip I: Connection   7

Trip II: Beauty   35

Trip III: Nurture   71

Trip IV: Novelty   119

Trip V: Independence   185

TRIP I: CONNECTION

"Le passere la sera intreccian voli
A noi d'intorno ancora. Oh resta qui."
Giosue' Carducci

The birds in the evenings braid flights
Among us still. Oh, stay here.

My favorite poem in the whole world is "*Davanti San Guido*" by Giosue' Carducci. He passes through his childhood Tuscany as a grown man, a poet. The cypresses recognize him and speak to him, they remind him of his youth and they appeal to him to stay. He listens to them, and engages in conversation with them, and he reminisces with them, but he doesn't, ultimately, *stay*.

SASSELLO

My son George and I walk through the pedestrian shopping street in Sassello and everything is exactly the same. Well, not everything: the butcher has moved across the street, but the shop still has the red curly plastic strand curtain to keep the flies out.

The bakery is still there, the Bellonotto.

The *tabacchino* is still there, with the ceramic sign above it, Tabacchi. They also carry newspapers and magazines and toys. They have a display of cheap toys hanging outside. And inside, it's the same people. I couldn't have told you what they looked like if you had asked, but now that I see them I recognize them.

And the Bar Gina is still there. It's a locale on a prominent corner, and like all Italian bars it's a bar but it's open and airy, and this one is famous for its ice cream, particularly fruit ice cream, made with fresh fruit in season like peach, raspberry and melon. The sign outside has a big ceramic ice cream cone, same as it always had. We walk inside and Gina is there, scooping ice cream. Of course. What else would she be doing? She is ancient, but she moves with energy. She keeps the ice cream in deep tubs, so she has to lean over and reach deep into the tubs, not an easy physical thing to do, but she has been doing it for decades and is doing it still. She's not personally a charmer, she doesn't do small talk, but she's a local legend.

We order two cones, and as she begins work on the first one a little bit chips off the edge. She sets it aside, and I tell her it's okay, I don't mind the little chip. She says no, she'll give us another one. As we walk away with our trophy cones, I turn around, and she has picked up the chipped one and is munching on it.

In the bigger square just outside the old town, the one with the parking spaces, are the stores that sell *amaretti*, almond macaroons that are the specialty here.

Back inside the village we walk up the other street. This one has the hardware store, with an outdoor display of brooms, gloves, knives, mats, watering cans, coffee makers, thermometers, umbrellas, and anything else you might need. There's a great Fellini film called I Vitelloni, in which an old woman walks into a small town store and asks for, "two little candles like the ones I bought last year." That's what this store is like. If you walked in and asked for two clothespins like the ones you bought last year, they would know what you mean, walk to the back, and come back with the clothespins you want. Then they would package them nicely for you.

Farther down is the shoe store. What was always remarkable about this store is that it had a giant shoe hanging outside. And this big shoe is still there, attracting shoppers. This single brown shoe is the length of three shoes. The shop carries a selection of sensible footwear of all kinds, arrayed in display cases and on boxes neatly arranged in rows. The sale items are in baskets, with the low prices advertised with hand-written signs. I have never bought shoes here and never will, but many must do.

George likes the big shoe. He will display regularly an interest in unexpected things, not the things I'm trying to share with him. But we share a like for the big shoe.

~.~.~

As a small child and later in high school we lived in Milan and spent the summers in Sassello. It's a little town in the Ligurian hinterland, hilly, surrounded by woods. The town is small but it has some stately buildings, some large churches, and shops.

I love Sassello.

I don't remember very much about the early days here, though we have pictures of them. What I think I remember I may have instead just seen in the pictures. My trip here today I will also recall from the pictures I'm taking.

My grandparents spent time here with us. My grandfather was an admiral and our next door neighbor was also an admiral, and I didn't really know what that meant, so I thought all old men were admirals.

I do recall that there was a big flower bed with dahlias and daisies. I have put daisies in my garden in New Jersey because of it, but they were overrun by black eyed Susans. There was a small chapel. There was also a large tree stump that my sister and I used as a table. My grandfather's sister remembered my sister and I offering her tasty *mangiarini* we had concocted on the tree stump, made of dirt and coffee grinds. Behind the house there was a grassy field with fruit trees.

I recall that there was a grape arbor in the garden, with a bench at one end. We parked the car at the other end of the arbor. One time my cousin Nino started the car and nearly took out the entire family.

From the house we went hiking in the woods, with the specific goal of mushroom picking. We were good mushroom pickers—porcini mushrooms primarily. We have a home movie of my mother holding an exceedingly large mushroom, turning it this way and that for display, the pride of the pick. Someone else's dog, a little caramel colored dog named Dick, pronounced Deek, accompanied us on our hikes.

My father worked in Milan during the week and came on the weekend. My grandfather would go into town in the morning, food shopping. He used to take me, and he called me his *nipotina prediletta*, his favorite granddaughter. I didn't know what it meant though I knew to be proud of the moniker. I'm not sure where that put my sister who was certainly as lovable as I, if not more. She may have been tiny at the time. I was a nice and well-mannered kid, a pleaser.

On Sundays we went to church at San Giovanni, a solitary beautiful church on a hilltop surrounded by a small park with a stone wall, benches, and a merry-go-round. My sister and I wore matching pink and white Sunday dresses, the same ones every Sunday, we only had the one good outfit. We weren't poor, I think the culture then was you only had what you needed. And you did need a good outfit for church, but not multiple ones.

Then we moved to Brazil and this particular part of my childhood ended.

~.~.~

We walk up to see our old house, a little outside of town. *Localita'* Colletto. A place without street names, just *localita'* Colletto. The house is still there of course, it looks exactly the same. There is no new construction around it, and no destruction. It's the same.

This was a summer place, but there was a couple that lived here year round, Ina and Paolo. Paolo worked for one of the *amaretti* makers, he drove a Vespa. For him a Vespa was not a cool 1960s means of transportation, it was an inexpensive and practical means of transportation. Ina helped out in the summer, she cleaned houses and sold the eggs from her chickens. If there is one reason I love chickens, it's Ina's chickens, roaming around. Ina and Paolo did not have any children, and Ina in particular was a great buddy to us, she would give us chewing gum, which was totally forbidden, our parents would never give us chewing gum.

We had two friends in Sassello, two girls the same age as my sister and I—Paola and Maria Elena. They spent their summers thirty meters from where we spent ours, and we spent hours and hours of every day together.

We walk by the steps where we used to sit. I expect to see them, I expect them to be there, but they're not. No one is. It's all the same, but it isn't.

~.~.~

Memory is a funny thing. I remember some things clearly, while other things, details really, I don't remember at all. But as I see those details again, the memories of them from back then come back. Things that I had forgotten I now remember, and vividly. The pattern of the paving stones of the road—stones cut about 2 by 2 inches square, arranged in interweaved semi-circles—is not something stored in any photograph and not something important enough to remember—it was not something I would even have actively noticed back then. But when I see it again, it's so characteristic of the place, I remember it now, seeing it again.

There are things I don't remember that turn out to exist. And then there are things that I thought I remembered that, on inspection, turn out to be different from what I remembered. Much of it is related to scale—things appear smaller. And where I remember things that are no longer verifiable, I have to remain wondering if my recollections are true.

~.~.~

How do you decide to embark on a trip? Some people just go, others plan perpetually and never act on their plans. In my case I went to a high school reunion of my American high school in Italy. The reunion was in New York, so it was easy for me to go. I realized then, and only then, that I hadn't been back to Italy in ten years and asked myself, "Why not go?" And, on a whim basically, I went. I went to reacquaint myself with Italy, and to show it to George for the first time.

My husband could have come, I'm not sure why he didn't. I don't think I asked him to, I don't think he asked to come. When he dropped us off at the airport he turned to me and said, as his last words, "If he is kidnapped, you demand to go along." Well, hopefully we will only have fun.

MY AUNT

When we first arrive in Italy, George's first trip, he is seven years old. We land in Milan early in the morning, rent a car, and drive down to my aunt's house in Liguria, on the coast. I have a map but I also know the way, it feels nice to know the way.

My aunt greets us when we arrive, she comes to the car and hugs us. She had met George once in America when she visited when he was a baby. He is a cute little blond American boy. My aunt is so happy to see us. I can't believe we're here. George can't believe it either, he is disconcerted. I won't realize until much later how strange everything is to him. He's my son, this should feel familiar to him, but it doesn't at all.

My aunt is a lovely person, she's beautiful and she likes to dress well. She's 80 now, and she still looks good in her clothes, she wears fashionable clothes. She is cheerful and tells funny stories. She loves to do stuff and see people, she's chatty. She's fun to be around. My uncle recently passed away after a long illness. They were married for nearly 60 years, and she is alone now. Her two sons, my cousins Gianni and Nino, who are quite a bit older than me, are good sons although busy men.

She wants to know what George eats. This will be a recurring nightmare for me as I navigate between his extreme fussiness and everyone else's complete determination to prepare for him what he likes. Which is nothing. And even what he does like, he doesn't like consistently. The fact that something is an Italian delicacy that someone went to some trouble to buy and cook it doesn't phase him one bit, "I don't want it."

"Just try a little bit."

"No."

He holds tight to what he knows, which is not much really, but he's holding on to it. It's all he's got.

She has rented a bicycle so George can learn to ride it. That's a funny thing to do, and I think it's a way for her to have something vested in him, he'll remember that he learned to ride with her.

I DID EVERYTHING RIGHT

There's a running gag in my family. When something goes wrong, I state, "I did everything right." I say it partly because that's me, I do things right, it's not my fault, and partly to pre-empt others making me feel bad, which is also me, eager to please and always hung up on what others think and feeling bad about disappointing.

I got good grades, went to college, got a job, got married, had a son, and I was always nice to everyone. Except maybe to my husband, but that's another story.

I did everything right. At this stage, there is not just one road not taken, there are many alternate ways, many turnoffs along the way. Unlike Robert Frost, I feel that I have generally taken the road more traveled by, though others looking in may think otherwise. I ended up in rural New Jersey from Milan, Italy, that's maybe not the road more traveled, though not all that exotic either. I've done and seen so many things, and I am where I am.

In going back to Italy, I see my past, it's so visible there, and in some ways I see what my life might have been if I had stayed there. But I didn't stay, and that's not my life. I am where I am.

Eric Kandel is a Nobel prize-winning neuroscientist, and he says in an interview in The New York Times, "You know, in the end, we are who we are. We're all part of what we've experienced." And that's true for me.

I did an exercise once where I listed the most significant events in my life, and then connected them to the values they represent. By doing that I came up with my values. Unknowing and then knowing, those are the things that guide me, and they are: connection, beauty, nurture, novelty and independence.

I'm not a planner, I never had tidy goals. I had, however, an unspoken plan in my head. If you live by your values, you move in the right direction. Because it was unspoken even to myself I always thought I was flighty—which is ironic enough, since I did everything right.

I got a fortune cookie just recently that says, "Be prepared to modify your plan." (The numbers are 23 28 34 36 45 and 9.)

I don't think so, I don't think I need to modify my nonexistent plan, I think my life evolves every day, I am what I've become, and I continue to become again and again.

THE LOCOMOTIVE

My cousin Nino was over for dinner last night and he invited us to ride in a locomotive. We have been here just a very short time, and we have this unusual opportunity. George loves trains, he has a big Thomas the Tank Engine set, so we happily accept. We meet him at the train, where the engine is used to move materials locally to the main train line. He tells us we can get aboard, and we do. The engine moves and George is spritzing excitement.

He is shown the button that operates the train whistle, and he is allowed to push it. George is whistling from the giant engine. He loves it. He does it over and over again until he's told to stop. Then he does it again. I tell him to stop. He does it again. He knows he can get away with it, what are we going to do to him? Push him off the train? Make him get off? He already got to ride it.

He will let me know later explicitly that he is fully aware of his powers, "There's nothing you can do to me." Which is true, I don't punish him, but he's a reasonable kid too.

And he does settle down.

All in all, we are on the locomotive for maybe ten minutes, we move a total of 100 meters, but this is a major thrill—he will remember it and refer to my cousin years later still as the guy with the train.

THE BEACH CLUB

We are on our way to spend a few days at a beach club in a small cove near Portofino. We stop for dinner in Santa Margherita, it's George and I, my aunt, and her grandson Fabrizio, Nino's son, who is a few years older than George and much more grown-up in his manner.

The first restaurant we stop at offers us a table at the back of the room, near the kitchen. It truly is the only free table, but my aunt declines it. She doesn't like it. So we leave. At 80, she retains her sense of self.

At the next place we get a table outside, among a sea of tables, close to the street. It's festive, it's a nice summer evening, it's almost electric, there are so many people eating, walking, driving by.

George must feel the electricity because he's wired. In fact, he is uncontrollable, I can't make him sit still. He knocks over his drink, I get up with him *"per fare due passi,"* to take a few steps, to try to talk him down, but I can't. He's wired.

We have pizza, I eat mine and most of his. Fabrizio had eyed the four-cheese pizza on the menu but he didn't order it. He's supposed to watch his diet, to eat reasonably, and the four-cheese pizza is too much. "I'll digest it tomorrow," he says, meaning it's a heavy food. It's supposed to be humorous, but it's not that funny coming from him. Coming from his father, as I'm sure it did originally, it would be funny, my cousin Nino is very funny. There's a whole segment of

Italian humor based on extreme exaggeration, and this is an example of it.

~.~.~

Liguria is a region poised to the sea. The mountains behind it are high and wooded, the sea is big and open, between the two are occasional thin stretches of flat ground, including some beaches. The beaches are small and sandy, but rocky at the water. It's hard to walk to and into the water. Most of the beaches are occupied by beach clubs—*bagni*—bathing establishments, many of them, side by side, elbow to elbow.

Each beach club has a distinctive color scheme and a catchy name such as Bagni Flora, Bagni Paolina, Bagni Sole e Mare, Bagni Surf Club, and Bagni Torino. The latter name I find hilarious, Torino is a big cold industrial city. Each one consists of changing shacks that can be rented for the day or by the season, chairs and umbrellas arranged in perfect rows. There's a snack bar and sometimes games like foosball and pinball machines. Some rent boats, and then there's the *boa*, a floating square 20 meters out, 60 feet, that you can swim to and sit on and dive from. And there's water to rinse your feet at the end of the day.

Some days the beach clubs put little signs out that they are sold out.

There is a whole tradition to the beach club scene. People choose one over the other based on intangibles—usually they know someone who goes there. They go every day, same routine, they sit for hours, they chat, they play cards, maybe they go home for lunch, or they eat there. There's a certain beauty to the beach clubs, their neatness, the colors, the predictability, year after year, day after day. I used to covet the beach club life when I was young. Although they're not clubs, they give you a sense of belonging. We went to the beach club with my aunt some, though mostly we went to Sassello. Now I can't imagine spending my summer that way. It's just not me.

Plus I don't like to pay the fees.

So George and I go to the public beach.

For every long sequence of beach clubs, there are a few arm lengths of public beach. The public beaches have to be there, they're legislated, but they're tiny. The public beaches have no pretty colors, no umbrellas, no place to change or rinse your feet, and no spare square of sand. They're usually very crowded and they don't have that feel, the part I coveted, of belonging. The crowd at the public beaches is not made up of regulars. It's out-of-towners down for the day and, it seems, Eastern Europeans.

But today we are guests of my aunt and we are going to a beach club, and a fancy one at that.

We enter the beach club with my aunt and Fabrizio. The beach is in a tiny cove so the beach club is mostly on decks attached to the rocks next to the beach. There is a tiny little actual sandy beach, and we have two chairs and an umbrella right on the beach, in the front row. This is a plum location, my aunt is treating and I'm sure it's very expensive.

This is a place where a great tan is very important. All the women wear tiny bikinis and some are even topless, and they lie in the sun all day every day. It looks spectacularly luscious as a life style, but I couldn't do it. I really couldn't. I had specifically thought I would go to the beach with George, I had thought of that as an appealing way to spend a vacation, but more than a couple of days would be too much for me and I think eventually for him too.

The lifeguard is a middle aged man, thin, and fully clothed. He is wearing white shorts, a blue polo shirt, and boat shoes. He has his own umbrella and chair on the beach. There seems to be no expectation that anyone will need to be saved. His umbrella and chair are strategically located at the edge of the beach club, right before the free beach. The free beach is small and overflowing and his true role in the enterprise I believe is to prevent the free beach bathers from encroaching on the expensive beach club sand.

There is a second fellow who looks like what I think a lifeguard should look like: young, hunky, and in swimming trunks. This young man is there to entertain the children. He runs games and contests of all kinds.

Fabrizio, who is 11 years old, is one of the bigger kids, he is confident and independent, and I call him the Mayor of the beach club. He collects sea creatures in a bucket with water in it, and he touches them. George is like a little yellow duckling, he follows Fabrizio everywhere, all day. And he calls out to him constantly, "Fabrizio!" "Fabrizio!" "Fabrizio!" At a certain point, Fabrizio gets a little annoyed and tries to shake him, but very graciously. George is little and he's friendly, and he has no idea he's getting on anyone's nerves, and he doesn't get the message, and will not be shaken. He stays with him. If Fabrizio stops short, George bumps into him.

In the games organized by the not-the-lifeguard, George plays along as best he can. Not-the-lifeguard tells Fabrizio to explain to George what he's supposed to do. George is klutzy and little and not competitive and he doesn't speak Italian, so he has no idea what's going on, but in all the pictures he looks perfectly delighted, with a big smile, and at the end of the day he has red scrapes all over his belly from jumping on and off the styrofoam floaters.

In addition to the lifeguard and not-the-lifeguard, there are many people working here, there's a reception/cashier, people working in the restaurant, and a woman who works the towels. They all hustle and are exceedingly attentive and courteous. The following year I will come here without my aunt, and—I'm guessing that because of the English and because George doesn't look much like me—they will think that I am the baby sitter, and they won't so much as look at me when I walk by. They will be completely rude. I never will go back again after that.

We have lunch at the beach club and Fabrizio orders the four-cheese pizza. I guess he feels he can digest it today, same day.

EREMO DEL DESERTO

We are going to the Madonna del Deserto, a place I had been once with my aunt and uncle many years ago. It is a monastery, and it's not in a desert but in deep, deep woods.

After some debate on how to get there, we decide to ask the gardener, a young man who is known to know everything—from the evidence, I can't conclude he knows everything, but I can assert that he knows this.

We are referring to the place incorrectly as the Madonna del Deserto, it's really the Eremo del Deserto. Yes, yes, yes, that's it. Eremo, schmeremo. Once we get that straightened out, so we are clear on where we really want to go, he directs us, "Take the road to Le Faie, and then turn right." Indeed. This is typical of Italian directions: they start at a point that's unknown, and then provide limited further instruction. Because everyone knows already how to get there, there's no culture of going places you don't know.

And in fact my aunt knows what he means, so we go. We are headed inland from the coast, uphill. As we turn off the more main road, the road gets narrower and more curvy, basically a one-lane two-way road where, because of the curves, you can only see a few meters in front of you. Harrowing. My aunt tells me to honk on the corners, that's how it's done. I feel it's not manly so I don't do it, until I get a good scare from an oncoming car, and then I get with the program, I do how it's done, I honk.

After many, many curves, we arrive. It's a plain fairly large building in an open spot in the woods. There is an old caretaker tending to the front of the building. We walk into the church, light a candle. There's a famous ivory crucifix here, and a small brochure tells its tale.

It was bought in India in 1641 by a Portuguese knight, the handiwork of a Catholic Indian. When the knight was returning home, his ship was attacked by pirates and he was brought to Algiers, where the crucifix was exhibited and mocked and physically hurt, whereby it bled. A Ligurian monk also prisoner in Algiers collected the funds to buy the crucifix, he kept it safe, and when he was released in 1643 he brought it to Genova, from where it ultimately went to the Deserto is 1646. Here it was maintained "with affection," the brochure says, which speaks to both the religious and personal nature of these relics. Twice, in 1799 and again in 1858, the crucifix left the location with the monks, later to return with the monks. The last return dates to 1955, and it and they have been here ever since.

Then we walk up a short Via Crucis, up a little incline in the woods. There's something about a Via Crucis that I like. It's not the spirituality of it, I'm not very spiritual, but there's something about it, the structure, the symbolism, the universality, the fact that in unexpected places you see a cross, then another cross, and you realize it's a Via Crucis. In Doylestown, Pennsylvania, there's a little garden next to the church with a Via Crucis. They're not crosses, they're scenes from the ordeal. You see one scene, then another scene, and you realize it's a Via Crucis.

We go in the little shop. My aunt buys my mother a little medallion and I buy two soaps. George has really no use for any of this. A building in the woods, what?

On the return home, we decide to proceed forward along the road rather than retracing our itinerary. The route forward will also take us back to the coast. The road continues to be eerily narrow and frightening. I honk constantly, one hand on the wheel, one hand on the horn—which is not easy to do.

We get to a little stream with a little room to park the car, so we stop. George loves the stream, finally something he can appreciate. We go to streams all the time in Bucks County, here is something familiar—finally!

THE BATTLE OF THE COUSINS' OLIVE OILS

My aunt gets her olive oil from a cousin on her father's side of the family who has olive groves in western Liguria, close to France. She is very proud of her olive oil, proud that it's so good and made by family. She loves to talk about it to anyone who will listen. She also gets an olive tapenade from her cousin that she serves on saltine crackers to accompany a white wine aperitif.

A cousin on her mother's side also has olive groves, these in Tuscany, and he brings her some olive oil to try. It's also very good, though possibly not quite as good, and much more expensive.

The first cousin wins.

SASSELLO

We go back to Sassello in the afternoon. For no reason other than I like to go there. We walk up to San Giovanni, a pretty church in a little park, up a little road, a little away from town, with a view of the wooded hills. The roof of the church has a curved pattern that's unique. To get up to it there are wide stone steps, and at the top of the steps, stone columns with a flame motif at the top. There are stone benches. I have a picture of my uncle sitting on one of the stone benches, and I take a picture of George sitting on the same one.

The front of the church is cobble stoned, and there are some tall trees around. It's one of the prettiest places I've ever seen, I love this place.

When we got back from Brazil as teenagers and moved back to Milan, we started coming back to Sassello in the summer again, to a different house right by the old one. The new house used to be occupied by a woman named Giustina who made mattresses. When we told someone where we lived we would say, "Where Giustina used to live, Giustina of the mattresses," and everyone would know exactly which house it was. She made mattresses stuffed with wool.

Our friends Paola and Maria Elena were still there, and we picked up our friendship where we had left it off. Sitting on the steps. This pattern of friendship has stayed with me all my life—just a very few really good friends. Sometimes I think I don't have enough friends, but I'm sure that if I wanted more friends I could get more. I really just want a few very good friends with whom I have many shared experiences.

On Sunday we would walk up to San Giovanni to attend mass, my sister and I and our two friends.

We did not usually have a car in Sassello, my father had the only car in the family, and he was in Milan during the week. We also didn't have a phone. We walked to the Bar Isaia when my mother had to make a phone call, they had a pay phone service. The Bar Isaia was on the main road, not in the town, it was pretty large, and it had parking outside. At times, it was a cool place where teenagers hung out and played foosball. At other times, it seems that no one went there, but it kept going, with its pay phone service, the only thing we ever went there for.

In the mornings in Sassello we would go food shopping in town. My mother sent us. She sent us because it was a battle, it was a task for the strong. Each little tiny shop was crowded, and there was an invisible queue, where you had to mentally account for who was ahead of you, and then be sure to request to be served when it was your turn. And anybody at any time, these meek looking ladies, would look to cut in front of you if you weren't quick enough. And then you'd have to call her on it, "*Scusi*, I was here first." The whole process is socially acceptable, it's acceptable to try to cut in front of someone, and it's acceptable to claim precedence. As long as it's claimed in a cool tone of voice. If you get heated then you're considered rude. Even if technically you're right.

In the afternoon we would go hiking or go splashing in a river, both things I still like to do today with George. Then we'd go into town to Bar Gina for ice cream.

In the evening we would sit on the steps and talk until dark. One year there was a soccer tournament in the evening, and Bar Gina fielded a team—that was the team we rooted for, we became rabid Bar Gina soccer fans, fundamentally on the strength of the ice cream, not because they had a better team. We'd walk home chanting after the games.

GIULIANA AND HER DAUGHTERS

I want to see my mother's friend, Giuliana. I know that she is extremely hard of hearing so I'm a bit hesitant about calling her, trying to explain who I am, so I decide instead to go by where she lives and see what happens.

This is my mother's college friend. They went to college together in the early 1950s, at the University of Genova. My mother was the only woman studying engineering, and Giuliana became a doctor. They still write to each other, long old-fashioned letters in which they discuss their families, their lives, and also politics, and recipes. Giuliana feels a little sorry for us because we don't have access to the ingredients required to cook properly. For example, we have regular artichokes and not the artichokes from Albenga. It's a sad state of affairs when you can't get artichokes from Albenga.

My mother wanted to study architecture but that would have entailed going to college in Torino, which was farther than her parents were willing to let her go. My sister and I went off to college in America from Brazil where we were again living at the time. This was in the early '80s, not really that much later, and it was still a pretty daring thing to do, and quite possibly degenerate.

Now Italian sons and daughters are big travelers. They believe it's important to learn English, that's the language of the world, and a useful language in a country heavily reliant on tourism. They are willing to travel abroad for extended periods of time to learn it. They tell their families that they are willing to make that sacrifice. And if they have fun and some great experiences, well, that's just a bonus. Not everyone of course can do this, but those that can, do, and Giuliana's grandchildren are among them.

Giuliana lives on a little square across from the beach in Celle Ligure. We spent time at the beach with them when we were all kids, my sister and I, and her three daughters. One time, we were playing around a rowboat and one of her daughters got stabbed by an oarlock and had to be taken to the hospital. I still remember that and I'm sure they do too.

George and I make our way over, it's early afternoon, which is a very bad time to try to visit anyone in Italy, though prime time for us. It's quite hot. I look up at her window and it's open. Do I ring the bell? Do I wait? How long would I wait? I'm very shy and this is an awkward situation. For the time being, I dilly dally. George wants to know what we're doing, and I really don't know what we're doing, and I don't know how to explain to him what we're doing. We're waiting. And feeling kind of silly.

We make our way to the beach, where her beach club is. I remember this being her beach club, and I don't even consider the possibility that she may have switched. The beach club has the little changing booths and the snack bar, the chairs and the umbrellas. It's pleasantly sleepy, a beach in the early afternoon. Suddenly I see Giuliana's eldest daughter walking. This is someone I haven't seen in many, many years, and I recognize her immediately. And she looks my way and recognizes me. As shocked as I am to run into her, she must be much more shocked than I am. She smiles, she hugs me, she keeps saying over and over that she recognized me right away.

I told her that I'm here for a few days and that I would like to see her mother. She says absolutely, and she takes us upstairs. Her mother does not recognize me quite as quickly, but she does after a moment, and is also very welcoming and warm and wonderful. She is a widow, her husband, also a doctor, passed away. Giuliana's second daughter is here too, and so are some grandchildren, and evidently I just missed the youngest daughter. They keep saying that over and over, they can't believe I just missed her.

George is of course dazed and confused. Who are these people? Why are they so gabby? And they are a gabby crowd, very cheerful. They want the children to practice their English with George, though it's unanimous: neither George nor the other children wants to do that.

We chat about this and that, about America, about them. I have a camera with me but for some reason I don't take any pictures. I think I'm just still nervous about the whole thing.

Eventually, we have to leave. We have dinner plans with my aunt, and George is nagging me that he wants to go, and he gets more and more insistent about it. I try to pretend he's not doing that, hoping they don't understand what he's saying. In fact, Giuliana doesn't understand but her daughters do, and he's little and they are sympathetic and they explain it to her, and she is sympathetic too. We say our good byes and we go.

HOME

At the airport in Milan there is a life-size statue of Harry Potter made out of Lego. This might make the trip for George. He has suffered, to his mind, quite a lot, but now he gets to gaze at this and be photographed next to it.

On the plane we watch a continuous loop of Jack Black in Nacho Libre for the eight hours.

When we get home my husband tells me has enjoyed living by himself and has decided to move out. The ultimate disconnection, my family disconnecting.

It will turn out that I too like living by myself. I dedicated so much time in my youth to ensuring I had a family, but now that whole thing seems less important, and that's very much because I have George, who is really the center of my universe.

~.~.~

We do go bike riding, George and I, on the bike trail along the Delaware River. In spite of my aunt's efforts, he is not an enthusiastic biker, he starts to request to turn around after about 100 yards. I create a whole Indiana Jones world for him, to entice him along, and it works. It involves ghost trains, native warrior canoes, a waterfall of doom, and the like.

I call the trail from Stockton down to Lambertville the Kathmandu to Lhasa run. This is clever of me because Kathmandu and Lhasa are in the Himalayas, they are not bikable, or so I think. I will read in The New Yorker about someone who met his future wife in Lhasa, as he was leaving on a bike ride to Kathmandu. People bike in the Himalayas. Proof positive that real life is stranger than fiction.

And my little fiction does work, it gets George to bike on the bike trail, through all the dangerous and exciting made-up landmarks. Though he doesn't like being away from home on an exotic vacation, I have to make home exotic for him to want to ride his bike.

TRIP II: BEAUTY

"Vedi come pacato e azzurro e' il mare,
Come ridente a lui discende is sol!"
Giosue' Carducci

You see how calm and blue the sea is,
How the sun lowers itself in it, smiling!

LIGURIA

Liguria is a long thin region that runs along the Mediterranean from France down to Tuscany. From the sea, the terrain goes uphill to fairly large mountains. There is very little flat ground, just a thin strip between the sea and the mountains. It's spectacularly beautiful: the sea is usually calm, the tiny towns are charming in their pastel colors, and the mountains behind it are forbidding and lovely at the same time. There is, however, no place to move.

There are only two roads that run the length of Liguria. One is the *autostrada*, this stretch of it is called the Autostrada dei Fiori. It's located up the hills in a sequence of tunnels and bridges: tunnel, bridge, tunnel, bridge, the entire length of Liguria. Each tunnel and each bridge has a name and a sign with the name. In parts the *autostrada* is close to the coast and easy to get to, in other parts it's quite a bit inland.

The other road that runs the length of Liguria is the Via Aurelia. It's the Roman road that went from Rome to France. It's still called the Via Aurelia. Why change a perfectly good name and possibly cause confusion? In places there is a *vecchia* Aurelia, an older stretch of road, a variation.

The road is somewhat improved from Roman times, but not really that much. It snakes along the coast, through the towns, people crossing it, motorcycles everywhere, cars double parked. But there are no other roads, it's the *autostrada* or the Via Aurelia.

Liguria is very lively. Because it's tightly packed along the coast, and it's a vacation destination, and there's a beach, and little shops, and there are so many motorcycles and people and flowers and palm trees, it's very lively, there's movement and sound everywhere. It's a little draining. Particularly when driving, you have to be alert all the time. There's an energy there that is unusual, even for Italy.

And there's no place to park, you have to keep moving. People have their obsessions, that they're attached to. My obsession is parking, and I'm attached to that obsession. I remember first and foremost of any place I go to, where I parked, whether I parked legally or illegally, how the parking situation affected my visit, whether I had to walk a long distance from the car, whether I was late as a result, whether the parking was timed so that I had to rush back, whether I paid for parking and how much it cost, whether I scratched the car pulling into the spot, whether I had to maneuver in or out, whether I parked in the shade or in the sun, and I remember those times when I doubted I could find my car again. I also remember when I couldn't find any parking at all and had to keep moving.

~.~.~

The traffic hubbub contrasts with my aunt's house, with her garden, that's very peaceful. Going from her house to the Ligurian streets is like watching a luxury car ad, where it's quiet inside the car with the windows rolled up, and noisy outside. Quiet inside, noisy outside, quiet inside ...

VARIGOTTI

There are two sides to Liguria, the Riviera di Levante, the eastern Riviera, literally the Riviera of the rising sun, which includes Portofino and the Cinque Terre and is more glamorous, and the Riviera di Ponente, the western Riviera, the Riviera of the setting sun, which is a little more low-key.

The town of Varigotti is in the western Riviera, and it's unusual among the local towns because its architecture is Saracen in style: the buildings are low and plain. It looks like a Sardinian town rather than a Ligurian one. We go to the beach here on a cloudy day, so we are two of the few people out there, George plays in the sand for a long time. I have pictures of him playing with no one else in the shot.

The beach is unusually large, and there are boats drawn up on it. We have ice cream on the way out.

There's not much to say about Varigotti. Anne Morrow Lindbergh, who flew all over the world with her husband Charles, believed that writing down an experience or an event made it more real, according to her daughter Reeve. Writing down this afternoon in Varigotti does that for me, an otherwise uneventful afternoon.

RITUALS

George can't sleep, and he cries. He's freaked out by it. And I can't calm him, I keep trying to tell him to relax, but he can't.

My aunt hears us talking, she realizes there's something going on. I tell her we can't sleep, that George is upset about it. She opens the *tapparelle* in her bedroom, the heavy roll-up window shades, and we step out on the balcony to look at the lights. There are lights all around us, it's like Christmas everywhere, plus the stars. George loves it, he stands out there looking all around, then we go back inside and to bed, and he falls asleep.

We will do this many nights, even when he doesn't have trouble sleeping, we go outside to look at the lights before bed.

We have another ritual where we tell each other how much we love each other, and we try to outdo one another. "I love you from here to here," pointing to one ear and then the other. "I love you from here to Genova and back." "I love you from here to a galaxy far, far away." And so on. This is ongoing, we will do this for years.

In the morning, we all wake up around the same time, and my aunt and I have a little tradition for the morning. She has a coffee maker in the hallway off the bedroom, and she makes coffee first thing, before she goes downstairs. She makes coffee for both of us, in little tiny cups, and she shares a few plain vanilla cookies that I dunk. It's hard to dunk in the little tiny cup. We sit on two chairs around my grandmother's vanity, and we chit chat about the day's plans, the weather as it impacts the day's plans, and the worries around the risks of the day's plans. My aunt knows I'm a grown woman who has done a lot of things on her own, but she still worries about me, and about all the terrible things that can befall me out there.

This routine is not breakfast, this is before breakfast which follows immediately afterwards downstairs. Breakfast involves a bigger cup with milk in the coffee, and more cookies, including bigger ones, *biscotti del lagaccio*, that are big and crumbly. They are a local tradition. George gets cereal, usually chocolate cereal, because he's American. Cereal is called *corn flakes* here, generically, and it exists. What don't exist are all sorts of other American breakfast foods like pancakes and waffles, there's no maple syrup. No one eats eggs for breakfast, or bacon, or potatoes. Italians also don't drink milk in glasses. If they do drink milk, they heat it up and maybe put chocolate in it.

I enjoy this utter domesticity. I sometimes wish my life was like this, made up of little domestic routines, but it's not, and that's probably a good thing really, I have choices and I can have a little bit of both the home and the rest of the world. Nonetheless, I find small domestic chores soothing, washing the dishes and folding laundry. I can put order in things.

For lunch we usually eat a meat dish, and for dinner a pasta dish. Both meals include a side dish with two vegetables from among zucchini, eggplant, peppers, carrots or string beans. There's fruit and coffee. Sometimes there's ice cream: coconut, pistachio and coffee ice cream—an odd set of flavors, but all good.

At night we lower all the *tapparelle*, all the heavy wooden roll blinds at the windows. They are rolled down using a thick strap placed vertically to the side of each window. They must be down or the *ladri* will come in, the burglars, who are always lurking just outside the windows, waiting for the night you forget to lower the *tapparelle*.

You can leave a little space between the wooden slats for some light to pass through, or shut them solid. I like the crack of light streaming through. And the crack of air. It's sweltering at night most of the time, with no air conditioning and the *tapparelle* down. But I don't want to be the one to let the *ladri* in, so I swelter.

LIVORNO

We are visiting my father's family on the Tuscan coast, in Livorno. This is a small city, of about 160,000 people, built as a key Tuscan port when the port of the city of Pisa was no longer navigable.

My uncle Nardo is my father's older brother. He is 1.90 meters tall, 6'3", very tall, and he played professional basketball in Italy in the 1950s. More accurately, it would have been professional basketball if they had gotten paid. They did not get paid, though there were sponsors who covered their travel expenses. The biggest sponsor was Fratelli Neri, who still today operates the tug boats in the port of Livorno. My uncle Nardo played for Livorno. Other teams were in Bologna, La Spezia, and other cities, not necessarily the major cities because basketball was relatively unknown at the time.

My father played basketball too but he was not tall like that and he became a referee. He still has the whistle and the little rule book.

My uncle gave me specific directions from the *autostrada* to arrive at his apartment building. At a specific intersection I am to call him so he can meet me downstairs and let me into the underground garage. Clockwork. My uncle, like my father, is an engineer and very precise. Unlike my father, who is wound tightly, my uncle is very low-key. The apartment building is nice, situated in a garden.

Upstairs there's a festive reception awaiting us: my aunt Ilaria and my cousins and their children. It's fascinating to see them, to see the children, to see who they look like, how they move, how they smile. There's a baby with enormous brown eyes under very long lashes, she's terribly beautiful. She becomes for George the epitome of cuteness, anything or anyone cute he will encounter he will compare in cuteness against this baby and invariably the baby will win.

I have brought some assorted gifts for the children and a bag of *amaretti* for my aunt, who likes them.

Their apartment is large and well decorated. They lived several years in England and bought many pieces of antique English furniture. My uncle also travelled for work all over the world and he has brought back assorted souvenirs, like a little silver ashtray shaped like a sombrero from Mexico. It looks nice on the coffee table.

They also have a big Brazilian wooden statue, a primitive stylized human form carved roughly from dark wood. This statue was ours, we brought it back from Brazil and it stood prominently in the entrance to our apartment in Milan. Somewhere along the way we gave it to them, and here it is looking at me.

This part of my family speaks with a great Tuscan accent. My father has this accent too, but he's the only one in our immediate family. Here they all use it. Compared to them I speak like a dork. And that's how I feel around them, though it's entirely my creation, I feel like the dorky cousin from America. In fact, they couldn't be nicer or more welcoming, and we have a lot of history in common, they also lived in Milan when we did, they also lived overseas for a time, and they visited us in the U.S.

We go out to lunch at a restaurant. This restaurant is along a canal in Livorno, and the locale inside has exposed brick walls and arched ceilings. It's nice and the food is excellent—seafood. Interestingly, next time I will see them, a year from now, they will remember what everyone ate. In George's case, *pasta al burro*, pasta with butter.

My cousin's husband asks my uncle about his basketball days. It's funny and typical of our family that even though they see each other I'm sure regularly, they don't usually talk about his basketball days. He quit basketball when his first child was born. We talk about her, that she was always cold as a baby, just as she's always cold now, as she's cold today on an overcast summer day.

The children range in age from the baby, who sleeps in her stroller, to the oldest girl, a poised teenager. The middle three include George, a slightly older girl and a younger boy, and all three are lively and quick—they are smart children, very alert. They run in and out of the restaurant, and I expect a judging reprimand from one of the waiters, but we don't get one, they are agreeable.

After lunch we go to the Ardenza, along the sea, and the kids ride on the carousel. The rides are bright and appealing, cars, animals, … the kids ride and ride and ride.

~.~.~

It's the next morning and uncle Nardo is planning a little outing with me and George. First we have a breakfast of cookies that George will recall much later as a great breakfast.

We drive to Montenero, a mountain near Livorno, in the area where my father and his brother lived during the war, World War II. Their mother died of disease early in the war, in 1941, something that I think affected my father deeply. He was only 10 years old, his brother just two years older. My father never talks about his mother, but he has always had a picture of her on his night table, always. It's an old fashioned black and white photo, a bit artistic, a profile. I can't tell from it what she looked like, it's hard to tell. My father looks a lot like his father, and his father had blue eyes, fairly unusual in Italy, and as genetics work, George got his blue eyes. He was also an only child, like George.

When the war came, even though my grandfather was older, he was called up, he was a captain in a field artillery unit. They had four cannons, each cannon had two caissons, and all of them were pulled by horses. Towards the end of the war, they ended up on the island of Sardinia, a dry windswept place, and eventually they ate their horses, which helped keep them alive. Being on Sardinia, such a remote place, kept them alive in other ways too, because the war largely happened elsewhere.

My father and his brother were raised during those years by their mother's family, their aunts, and since Livorno was a port town and was bombed, they moved to Castelnuovo della Misericordia, behind Montenero. For a while they attended different schools, 5 kilometers (about 3 miles) in opposite directions. My uncle rode a bicycle to school, he carried my father on the bicycle halfway to his school in Rosignano, then my father continued on foot, and my uncle rode back and on to his own school in Quercianella. After a few months of this routine, the Germans came into the area and the school was closed. The boys were given exams in the church, and they all were promoted into the next school year.

My father kept busy repairing bicycles and cooking pots. He still likes to repair things, to tinker, meticulously. For a long period of time the boys had no news of their father, or he of them, as they were on opposite sides of the front, but eventually the war ended and he came home.

So here we are in Montenero with my uncle, and George is whining. This is not entertaining for him. There is a church here, a Santuario, and inside there's a very large collection of *ex voto* pictures. Each one depicts an accident that happened to someone, and for surviving the accident the person is thankful. What's fascinating is that the accidents are generally mundane, people falling off things, being hit, bitten by a dog, and the like. Each picture illustrates the accident itself as it's happening, the falling person in midair. George doesn't really get them, and I think if he were a little older he would appreciate them perhaps almost as cartoon happenings. They're very folksy and with so many all around us, it's scary to think how many bad things can happen, I find it a little morbid, but in fact I believe the art celebrates the faith in God's protection, and it's touching to see that people stopped to give thanks.

After Montenero we go back to the carousel for a few more rides, this is the entertainment that is sure to entertain every time, and it does.

We go back to the apartment for lunch, and Ilaria has made *pasta al burro* for George, a meal that he would normally eat, but woe, she has put grated cheese on it, so he pushes it aside. I want to shake him, but I try to make light of what a little twit he is and I eat the pasta myself. It's very good, lots of cheese. I wish people wouldn't make him special food because he doesn't appreciate the gesture at all, but they do, because they're kind.

After lunch we depart. I'm sorry to leave this part of my family that I see so rarely. I do love them and especially my uncle Nardo, who is a gentle soul. I think that maybe from his great height he sees things differently.

CINQUE TERRE

On the map the Cinque Terre look to be just off the *autostrada*. If we were crows, and we could fly as they do, we could get there pretty quickly, flying straight, but we are on a Ligurian road. The Cinque Terre are in Liguria. The road winds down the mountain, then up again, then down again. It takes a long time.

We go through a tunnel that has a sign at the entrance, "*Accendere i fari in galleria*," turn on the headlights in the tunnel. All tunnels in Italy used to have these signs, but now the tunnels themselves are lit, and the signs are all gone. This one seems to be the only one left. I take a picture of the sign.

We finally get down to Monterosso, one of the Cinque Terre. We park illegally because I can't find a legal spot.

The town is full of tourists, including many American ones. The Ligurian coast towns usually have Italian tourists, not American ones, but this area is famous in America too. The man who sells us ice cream thinks we are Americans initially, and I go out of my way to be at my most Italian.

We stroll around, there's a newer part of town, where we are parked, and an older part. We walk through a tunnel to get to the older part, which is very cute, with the usual cheerful shops selling beach stuff. We are parked illegally so we can't really stay too long. Which is too bad because there is a long walking trail in the hills among the olive trees and lemon groves, the Via dell'Amore.

This is a place to come back to—in the winter. Many years ago, I came here with my husband in the wintertime, the weather was mild, the only other visitors were Italians on a weekend outing, wearing heavy winter coats. We walked on the trail a bit, among the olive groves and lemon trees. When I got home I planted lemon seeds from a supermarket lemon in pots and got little lemon trees. I still have them, they've never made any lemons.

ITALIAN TELEVISION

George had told me, when I told him we were going to Italy, "If they don't have Cartoon Network in English, I'm coming right back home."

I learned Portuguese watching TV in Brazil. I watched *Os Monkees, Jeannie e' um Genio* and *Perdidos no Espaço*. I was hoping very much that he would learn some Italian, accidentally, unwittingly, by watching TV.

But here's what I did not know: you can watch Cartoon Network in English in Italy! I did not travel 4,000 miles to have George sit and watch Cartoon Network in English. He can do that at home. But everyone is so gracious and puts it on for him, and eventually he'll learn to do it himself.

The one bit of Italian that he does pick up is the pronunciation, the flat way Italians pronounce words, and he catches on that there are many English words used in Italian, pronounced with the flat Italian pronunciation, and he likes to do that. He likes to say English words with an Italian pronunciation. And I will say, since that's all I got, that that's something.

My aunt's favorite show on TV is called Renegade. That's the Italian name. It's an American show starring Lorenzo Lamas as a bounty hunter who also, ironically enough, is a fugitive from justice. He is of course innocent and trying to clear his name. In the meantime he drives around town, somewhere out West, on a super cool motorcycle with his long hair blowing behind him—risky behavior for a wanted man, but appealing to older Italian ladies evidently.

Her other favorite show, and the favorite of her cousin Paolo, is Walker Texas Ranger—no plot complexities and lots of kicks.

CAMOGLI AND ZOAGLI

Camogli is a fairly frequently photographed town, there are tall skinny pastel colored buildings lined up like toy soldiers along the beach. At the far end there's a church perched on a rock right at the water's edge, which is unusual. Usually the church is nestled inside the town. Beyond the church, the beach ends and there's a tiny harbor full of fishing boats.

It's a quiet weekday and there are not many people around. We walk a bit, George gets a Coke, we buy some focaccia, and then we leave. We go up into the hills, park illegally as usual, and here too there are extensive walking trails that we don't have time for today. I hope to come back.

I have never been to Zoagli, so I stop. We park along the Aurelia, legally, high above the town, and walk down. We pass a nun sitting reading a book. I am curious about what she's reading but I don't ask.

We get to town, there's a round square, with a tall railroad overpass along one end of it, like a geometrical tangent. The train goes by on the overpass periodically. This is a big plus for George, having a train barge through directly overhead is way cool, and for the people there it seems to be a non-event, it doesn't seem to bother them.

We have some focaccia and an ice cream, and we sit on the beach for a little bit. The beach is small and rocky, and it's on the other side of the railroad overpass. You walk from the square, under the train tracks, to the beach, and the whole distance is small, it's all right there, with the train overhead.

PORTOFINO

We are going to dinner in Portofino with my cousin Nino, his wife and their son Fabrizio, who is a few years older than George. We get there fairly early. They're coming from work, from Genova. We sit at an outdoor restaurant right on the harbor, under umbrellas, as the evening slowly turns to night. The lights go on, and the moon rises.

Presently it starts to rain. The waiters move the umbrellas to cover us and the table better. We stay seated and continue eating, and then the rain stops. It was just a brief shower. Nino's wife is cold, she's a tiny thing and she's always cold. I'm used to colder weather so I tend to ignore the slight chill.

After dinner we get ice cream at another place and eat it in the *piazzetta*, looking out at the harbor. Nino's son runs into some kids he knows and they chat.

At the mouth of the harbor there is a small hill, the Punta di Portofino. At the top of the hill is a castle, Castello Brown. With the moon in the sky the castle looks spooky. George is a bit thrilled by it, what a magical evening.

Leaving town we drive past a line of cars waiting to drive into Portofino. Every time a car leaves, another one can enter the town.

~.~.~

We are going to visit Castello Brown—in the daytime. We walk up the hill bright and early. We walk by the church of St. George, who is the patron saint of Portofino. Throughout the town there are ceramic medallions depicting St. George in various dragon-slaying poses. The church sits on a site believed to have had a roman temple, according to a brochure in English we pick up at the castle. Pliny the Elder, or as the brochure says, Pliny the Old, wrote about the area in Roman times. We get to Castello Brown before it opens and we have to wait.

The castle is something less than a castle and something more than a villa. It was originally a fortification, going back at least to the 1400s, to protect the sheltered harbor. In the late 1800s the castle was bought by an English man named Montague Yeats Brown for 7,000 *lire*. Mr. Brown turned the building into a residence that stayed in his family until it was sold to the town in 1961.

We walk up steps through gardens to get there. Inside it's sparse. There are pictures of famous people who have visited. And most spectacularly there are beautiful terraces with wide views down to Portofino and out to sea. This would have been a beautiful home with a beautiful garden. It is a little spooky still, even in the daytime, isolated up high on this hill.

PLAYGROUNDS

I am starting to get an inkling of how disconcerting everything in Italy is to George. It has taken me a long time. He said to me once when he was little and I was not responding to him as he wished, "You're my mother, why don't you know my feelings?" I have not known his feelings well enough. To him, everything in Italy is foreign, in the sense of the word that's not about national borders but about strangeness, bad strangeness.

One thing that is familiar is playgrounds. In America too, each playground is unique. One has the bigger jungle gym, one has the little space shuttle on springs you can ride. But each is clearly a playground. He can understand the differences among playgrounds, and in fact he's selective about which playgrounds are worth it, but he knows a playground when he sees it. There are playgrounds in Italy!

In fact, there is one in Celle that we came to last year. And here we are back to it. Not only is it a playground, something within his world view, but it's a playground he's been to before. And that is cause for joy. He wants to stay here for a long time.

There are other children too, there's that playground atmosphere of relaxation that you find even in the middle of New York City. The area is enclosed, the parents sit, the children play. We have come 4,000 miles to see-saw. But that's okay. I want George to see new things, but I also want him to absorb the life, and the playground constitutes that part of the experience: here is regular life, in Italy. We can soak it in.

We pick up ice cream at an ice cream shop near the playground to take back to my aunt's. This is not an officially sanctioned ice cream shop, but I think the ice cream is very good. And grudgingly my aunt will agree.

We have parked the car uphill a little ways because, as usual, there's no place to park. As we walk back up to it, a car accosts us. My antenna goes up, what does this guy want? He asks, "Are you leaving?" He wants my parking space! I tell him yes, we are just up ahead, and I point to the car. He says, approvingly, "It's a good position." He says it like I offered him a job, he thanks me profusely. He cracks me up, and I leave him to occupy the fantastic parking space.

MARKET DAY

Monday is market day in Savona. Market day in Varazze is Saturday. It's not written anywhere, you just know. And once you know, you can count on it forever.

The market has everything, fruits and vegetables, cheese, aprons, sweaters, shoes, candy, scarves, herbs, tablecloths, toys, salame, pretty much everything—at good prices. This is not a fancy market, like a farmer's market in America, with high organic prices, this is a market of useful everyday stuff, cheap.

Every vendor is highly specialized. Each one sells its own thing only.

The people who come into town for market day are called *beciancilli* here, not a real Italian word. It's pronounced bay-chon-cheely. It's not a complimentary term.

Market day is like so many other things in Italy that are so ingrained that they exist invisibly. They just are. You don't realize how potent culture is when you are inside of it. When you step outside, it's conversely so visible and so mystifying. Miranda Kennedy writes at length about India and their cultural norms, and they seem so illogical to us, but they are felt deeply by the Indians themselves.

Being Italian myself, I step into the culture naturally, and I have a hard time identifying Italian cultural norms specifically.

Italians are very family-oriented, as everyone knows. They're not particularly community-minded. Churches are to attend and then go home, there are few social events attached to church going. Italians don't use public libraries. They don't have social clubs. Or fraternities. College does not entail the communal living arrangements that are common with dorms.

Italians are very polite with each other, they address each other formally always, using the third person singular, much as the French use the second person plural. They express themselves crisply and judge and reprimand freely, but always politely. When you walk into a store in Italy, that store is often owned by the person working in it, it's that person's livelihood. You are expected to engage with the storekeeper and to buy something.

Italians don't strike up conversations with strangers, but if you have any relation or business with them, they converse. It's not polite to ask personal questions.

Italians don't put screens on the windows and they like fresh food, they do their food shopping daily. In fact, they are overwhelmingly very particular about their food.

When I was growing up it was very important to wear an undershirt, a *canottiera*, and I think people still wear them. It was also important to always wear shoes, to keep your feet warm. Still today, no one in Italy walks into someone's house and takes off his or her shoes, other than George who leaves his shoes everywhere.

On the other hand, there are things common to Americans that don't register at all in Italy. In Italy no one has to be told not to eat in stores, or to wear shoes and shirts for that matter. When my aunt Ilaria visited us in New Jersey, she asked, "Who eats in stores?" Who would do such a thing? No one would dream of bringing his own wine to a restaurant, or to ask for a doggie bag. Nor do you usually need a doggie bag because portions are reasonably sized to be eaten at one sitting, they are not gargantuan.

Italians are more modest and moderate in what they own and do. They have a more limited scope of ambition, but they are not wallflowers either, they enjoy themselves and are accomplished. They seem more content, they live in their world and appreciate it.

These are my impressions. They may well be completely wrong.

SAVONA

Olivia has invited us to visit with her in Savona. She will bring Baldo along, a child who is just a little older than George and speaks English.

Savona is my mother's home town. It's more than a town, it's a small city of around 60,000 inhabitants, with four- and five-story buildings, and one taller one known as the *grattacielo*, the skyscraper. It's maybe twenty stories tall and very '60ish in appearance. There is now a second tall building, all green glass, next to the commercial harbor. In the old days, only cargo ships docked here, but more recently cruise ships do too.

On the way into town, we pass the building where my grandparents lived. It looks out over the port. We used to watch the ships coming in and going out of the port from the window, with the tugboats and the little gray *pilotina*, the pilot boat. My grandparents had a great apartment, large but very poorly laid out, with lots of rooms all off a central large hall. We mostly used the kitchen, which was small, and one room, the *saletta*. There was also a *salotto*, which was a formal sitting area, and a dining room, and only two bedrooms, one with a dressing room, plus lots of little hidden closets and a huge bathroom. It was a very cool place.

The apartment had shutters on the windows, *persiane*. The shutters had horizontal slits in them, from top to bottom. In the room where we slept, light would come through the slits when a car went by in the street, and hit the ceiling, and the light stripes would slide across the ceiling as the car moved. It was a magical light show.

The building was against a hill, so that there was a garden even though the apartment was on the third floor. The garden had formal flower beds, each one limited by rough faux stone, with gravel walks in between. Some of the flower beds were in the sun, with roses, tulips and geraniums. And some were hidden behind huge azaleas and hydrangeas. There was a kumquat tree and a single enormous palm tree in a round flower bed. There was a wisteria arbor with a bench under it. There was also an old slate tub where someone would have washed clothing in the old days. And at the top, raspberry bushes. This was a most fantastic garden, not very big but lovely. We played croquet, my sister and I, on the gravel walks. We would set up elaborate courses.

We pass the building and meet Olivia, and she has plans for us, she wants to take us to a bookstore to buy us a book and then to her apartment, where I've never been, for tea. Somehow, maybe because I don't want her to buy us a book, I suggest I would like to go to the Priamar, a fortress along the sea that has been opened to visitors. I don't realize that her own plans are fast, and that whatever I suggest will not replace any activity but be added to it, so we end up with a packed afternoon.

The walk to the Priamar is much longer than I anticipated. Olivia is small but she walks pretty fast, and the kids talk and laugh, George is excited to have a friend in Baldo.

The Priamar is a sixteenth century fortress built on a site that was inhabited much earlier, going back to 500 BC. We walk up into the fortress, and then within it. It's huge, with many interior courtyards, and a wonderful view from the top. There's a small canteen, where we stop for a soda. There's a wedding going on here today, that's the type of place that this is.

After the Priamar, we go to the bookstore. This is where I realize that the original plans are still all in place. I don't want her to buy us a book, but she insists and I find one about old Savona that I think my mother will like.

Then we go to Olivia's apartment. She has a very cool apartment, a duplex on two floors—a combination of her apartment and the one that belonged to her parents, who have both died. The lower floor is the main apartment, with a large room, and other rooms off of it. Upstairs is a room designed by her architect friend. Her friend is a huge admirer of Frank Lloyd Wright. In fact, George and I will visit the Frank Lloyd Wright exhibit at the Guggenheim in New York, just to tell Olivia about it. The upstairs looks like a Frank Lloyd Wright interior, with built-in wooden details, it's really very cool and—although I knew about it—really cooler than I expected. She serves us tea and cookies, a lovely spread. The sun is streaming through the window, and there's a lovely garden downstairs.

GOLDFISH

George enjoys feeding my aunt's goldfish. There's a little routine around that. The fish food is behind the couch, the fish are outside in a pond in a little grotto.

When he sprinkles the food into the water, the fish come swimming, it's fun.

Martha Gellhorn referred to her husband Ernest Hemingway as UC in her writing, Unwilling Companion.

George has been accompanying me oftentimes unwillingly but with spritzes of pure joy, and the goldfish are a source of joy.

My aunt is very proud of her fish. Her neighbors have fish, but theirs get picked off by the seagulls—hers do not, probably because the grotto's overhang prevents the seagulls from dive bombing.

MILANO

I spent the better part of my high school days walking around Milan. Walking being the operative word. I have never driven in Milan. I know my way walking around downtown like the back of my hand. I know every street downtown, and I have no doubt that it's all exactly as it was. Downtown. When I get downtown.

As I come off the *autostrada*, I follow the *centro citta'* signs with the little bull's eye target, follow them diligently until the signer deems we're close enough, and they disappear. I am somewhere between the countryside surrounding Milan and the *centro citta'*. The part of Milan, between the countryside and the *centro citta'* all looks the same. I don't recognize any of the street names. I don't know where I am. I'm tense and George can tell.

"*Mamma?*"

"Yes, George."

"Are we lost?"

"We're not lost. I just don't know where we are."

"Uhm, doesn't that mean we're lost?"

It's Sunday morning, there is not much traffic around, which is good, and there are not many people either. I see a couple walking a little dog down the street. What I specifically want to ask is, "Can you point me to somewhere that I know? I would like to be someplace that I know, and I can take it from there."

"*Scusi, per cortesia*, can you point me to Piazza Cavour?"

The couple is extremely gracious, and takes their time to direct me. It turns out we're not that far really. I find a place to park off Via Senato. Milan has three loops, the *circonvallazione esterna*, the middle loop, and the *circonvallazione interna*, which is in part Via Senato. We're good. I know where we are. I can walk now, I know my way around, I can leave the car, and I can briefly relive my time here.

Milan is a nice city, a little gray perhaps, very staid, not quaint really. It does have some superb sites: the Scala, which is the opera house, the Duomo, and the Castello Sforzesco. It also has the fashion district, Via Montenapoleone, glamorous in a very undertsated way. My grandparents used to live on a cross street, Via Gesu'. There is now a Four Seasons hotel across the street from their building. My parents got married in a church on Via Manzoni. I take a picture of George standing in front of the church.

The trams go by. Milan is served by trams. They were green when I was a kid, now they're orange. I point them out to George, and he thinks they're pretty cool. I show him the number one tram that goes down Via Manzoni.

I tell him, "See, the number one, it's the king of trams." Kind of like Thomas is number one and the main train character.

We head to the Duomo and go inside. It's huge. I don't really recall the inside, I don't think I spent much time inside. The Duomo has a gold *madonnina* above it, the symbol of Milan.

We walk to the Castello Sforzesco. It's the castle of the Sforza family that ruled Milan during the Renaissance. Leonardo lived here when he worked in Milan. George's piano teacher is named Mrs. Sforza.

This is a huge brick castle, absolutely huge. We go to the museum inside. Among many other things, there's a Pieta' by Michelangelo. I explain to George that this is a very famous statue. He gets tired of me telling him how famous everything is.

There's an Egyptian part to the museum. We had been to the Metropolitan in New York, which has a huge Egyptian collection, and George was disappointed that the mummies were still wrapped. In Milan, there's the inside of the mummy on display, the dead body.

George says, "Ew, that's gross."

"Well, you wanted to see the inside of the mummy, there it is."

Years later we will go see a King Tut exhibit in New York where there is a reproduction of King Tut's dead body and George will refuse to look at it. You think you want to see a mummified body until you see one, then you don't want to see it anymore.

As we leave the castle I point out more trams. There are older trams and newer long articulated ones. He really likes the trams. I consider taking a ride but decide to leave it for another time. Another time? We sit in Piazza Cordusio, a major tram hub, a convergence of several lines, and we stay for an hour—watching the trams go by.

I show George again the number one, the king of trams. He tells me, "No, it can't be a king, because there's more than one. I've seen more than one go by." So much for trying to tell him a story.

This happens to be about a block from where the American School of Milan upper school used to be. In the subway there used to be a record store. While I was never a music aficionado, I was very much an aficionado of my boyfriend at the time, and we spent many afternoons in that underground record store.

The people I went to high school with, the Americans who lived in Milan in the 1970s, remember the city fondly. They remember the freedom of walking around the town, taking the trams anywhere, and I remember those times as well, I remember doing that, spending time doing nothing, going anywhere. They remember getting caught in political demonstrations. I was overly protected, I wasn't allowed to get caught in demonstrations, so I missed that part, which was a big part of Milan in the 1970s.

Milan has one of the most famous theaters in the world, one of the most famous cathedrals, a huge castle, it's home to a fabulous fashion hub, but most excitingly to George it has many, many super cool trams.

Tomorrow we are leaving to go home.

NEW HOPE

It's a sweltering July 100-degree day, so we go to Bowman's Hill Wildflower Preserve just south of New Hope because it's wooded and so it's in the shade.

"Can we go in the visitor center? Can we go in the visitor center?"

"Okay."

The lady at the desk gives us a map of the site and a guide to help identify the flowers currently in bloom. It's a clever guide, it includes the color of the flower, the height of the plant, and the location or locations in the Preserve. She tells us it had been updated that morning as if it was fresh food.

She also tells us about the bird watching area with, she says, cushioned seating—a selling point. And she tells us about the collection of birds in the basement.

We linger at the bird watching station, where bird feeders are hung outside big picture windows. It's a lovely spot. I happen to look down at a small plaque on the window sill and it thanks supporters of the bird watching site, including the educational support of my former boss. I call to George to come quick and he does.

"Look. Look who's mentioned?"

"I thought you had seen a bird."

He would specifically not want me to refer to him as my old boss, why I referred to him as my former boss. He is an avid bird photographer. I will have to tell him about our visit.

We go downstairs to the bird exhibit and it's quite a bit more exciting than given credit for. It contains many bird's nests and eggs, as well as quite a number of stuffed birds. It's organized by habitat. The nests are so cool, all different nests of different sizes made of different types and sizes of sticks and leaves.

We finally go outside, and we use the map to guide us. The map makes the place look huge, with many different trails, but in fact it's not that large—the trails are very close to each other. And even in the shade it's very hot.

We sit on a bench and a couple walks by and the man says, "Too bad this bench is already taken."

I offer to relinquish it to him, and he says, "No worries. There's a bench every twenty feet." He smiles.

I turn my head and sure enough, there's a bench not far away.

George wants to know, "How long is a foot?"

"It's longer than your foot. If you bend your arm at the elbow and make a fist, it's about the distance from your elbow to your knuckles." He assumes the bent-elbow-fisted position, walks toward the bench, and along the way counts the arm increments. He's actually covering more ground than he thinks.

He gets to the bench and comes back to announce, "Actually, it's twenty-four feet away." He may be a future scientist, observing and experimenting.

~.~.~

On the way home we stop at the French bakery in New Hope. This bakery is so French that they have Asterix books for the customers to read. In French. We started one of the books on a prior visit, me reading and doing simultaneous translation from the French.

George reminds us, "We're on page 12."

TRIP III: NURTURE

"Intesi allora che i cipressi e il sole
Una gentil pietade avean di me."
                    Giosue' Carducci

I realized then that the cypress and the sun
Felt a gentle pity for me.

FERRAGOSTO

August 15th is a holiday in Italy. It's a religious holiday that has become an occasion to celebrate a bit, the way Italians celebrate, with a nice meal and some friends and family. I have arrived in time for Ferragosto this year because my aunt raves about the fireworks. There's the added bonus that they can be seen from her house.

In the old days, she used to throw a big party at Ferragosto. I was able to attend one year. There were tables in the garden and many guests, twenty or so guests, for a sit-down dinner, which is a pretty big party. She served lobster, this was the high point of the meal, caught by my uncle. She would freeze them until she had enough for the party, a gesture of planning and generosity and grand living all in one.

My uncle used to fish, he had a fishing boat and a fisherman buddy, and he fished off the coast. This he did for recreation, but he did it his whole life, he would set nets out in the evening and go back very early in the morning to pull them up. He had the license required to do this. And he set lobster traps. Italian lobsters are different than the New England ones, they don't have the big claws.

That year I helped with the *frutti di bosco* mix, the mixed berries. She said to me the next day, "There were some stems on them." I replied, "Oh, I didn't remove any stems."

This year the guests are George and I, her cousin Ginevra with Baldo, the little boy who is friends with George from a prior trip, my aunt's other cousin Paolo, and our friend Olivia. It's a nice gathering but I'm a little sad for my aunt that her big party of Ferragosto is reduced to this. She, on the other hand, seems completely happy. She has an uncanny ability to be very pleased with her circumstances that I envy very much, plagued as I tend to be by insecurities. She's having a Ferragosto party with several guests, two of whom came all the way from America, and she can provide a fireworks display from her house. As far as she's concerned, this is the best party!

She has bought each of the boys a building block car so they can amuse themselves while they wait for the fireworks. They are building furiously inside as we sit outside. Later the boys come out and Ginevra tells Baldo, "Help George with his car, he's younger than you."

Baldo replies, "Actually he already finished his. He's really good at this." George is good at following the building instructions, he really is quite able in that area.

One of the things I don't like about fireworks, though I love fireworks, is waiting for them to start. It's always excruciating to me. You know you have to wait until dark, you know that it has to be dark, but still it's hard to wait. And in the summer in northern Italy it gets dark late. Eventually it does get dark, the fireworks should start soon. They should. Start. Soon. They should. Start. Soon. Not so much. They start around 11 o'clock. So late!

They are pretty, though not really all that close to my aunt's house. Paolo makes the definitive assessment saying at their conclusion that they are better than those in Savona. Seal of approval.

MARIA'S STORY

Two years ago Maria had stopped by my aunt's house with a friend who wanted to sell my aunt a huge lot of porcini mushrooms. Huge being several dozen, which is a lot of mushrooms considering they are found one by one, growing wild, in the woods. They had called first to lay the groundwork.

Maria did some housecleaning for my aunt many years ago, she's a very hard working woman, a real salt of the earth type. Somewhere along the way they had a bit of a falling out as a result of some mutual stubbornness I believe, I don't know the specifics. Since then, they've had a *rapprochement*, their new relationship is based on their long standing mutual need and appreciation tempered by a balance of power, realpolitik. Maria helps my aunt out and refuses to be paid. My aunt repays her by buying gifts for Maria's grandchildren. And when Maria has a friend who wants to sell several dozen mushrooms, my aunt buys them.

This is what makes Italy function. People live in the same place for generations, and interact with the same people, they are part of a web. I think it's what sustains the country. The politics are dysfunctional, but everyone creates a web that fills their needs and that's how things get done.

Maria is back today for a quick visit, and my aunt nudges her, "Tell her what happened to you, your accident."

"What happened?" I ask.

And she proceeds to tell me, in many, many words, her terrible adventure—with a happy ending. This is Maria's story, condensed here, possibly unfairly because to her it was a very long happening, requiring many, many words. Maria was coming home in the evening on her *motorino*, her motorbike. There was a detour, she was detoured to the road to Gameragna. She tells me this as if she were saying, "The Holland tunnel was closed, I had to take the Lincoln," like it's an obvious detour. I had never heard of Gameragna, or knew of the road, or knew that the road could constitute a detour off the Aurelia. There is only the one road in Liguria, the Via Aurelia, along the coast. All other roads go into the hills, and the road to Gameragna therefore is in the hills. It was dark, the road was curvy, Maria rode into a ditch. A big ditch. The side of the ditch had been "improved" with a cement wall, and she couldn't get out. It was cold. She screamed but no one heard her. She stayed awake all night, worried about falling asleep in case she had a concussion, alone in the ditch. It must have been quite frightening, though she's a tough person and displayed quite the presence of mind through the whole thing.

In the morning she started screaming again. Someone drove by, this fellow was smoking, so he had his car window rolled down, and he heard her. He stopped the car, and he called to her, asking who was down there. She said, "Maria."

He asked her, "What happened?"

"*Sun couta*," she replied—Savonese for, "I fell."

It took a rescuer from the fire department quite a while to pull her out.

And she ended her story by saying, "Someone should write a book about it." It's not a whole book, but it's in a book, Maria's story.

MADONNA DELLA GUARDIA

There is a little church at the tippy top of a barren hill, overlooking the sea, all by itself, lit up at night, it's called the Madonna della Guardia. Going to that church seems like a cool thing to do, a worthwhile endeavor, a destination. I have seen the sign for it on the Aurelia, I know where to go. We take off in the car, drive up a curvy road among houses and buildings, but not for long. Soon the houses end and the road ends, with a little place to leave the car. We are nowhere near the church, and from here on, it's going to be on foot on a dirt road.

George sees the barren road in the beating sun, processes the situation accurately and immediately, and starts to register complaints with the management. I try to be positive and to encourage him on. He is not open to positive encouragement, but we start off regardless. I can't see the church from the road—a fairly flat road though we are going to have to gain altitude—that winds around the mountain. I give myself some positive encouragement and I do find myself receptive.

This section of mountain was damaged by fire, an *incendio*, which sounds like a much more apocalyptic event than a mere fire, and that's why it's so barren. But the mountain is slowly springing back to new plant life. It's lovely to see up close, nature doing its thing. There's a certain purity to walking in open space instead of the woods. The view, even from just a short way up, is beautiful: the sea, the coast, all the way to Savona.

George becomes more insistent in his complaints, resorting now to tears. He is crying. And he is so cute when he cries.

When he was little and something relatively horrible happened to him, such as a shoelace untied, or a missing toy, he would wonder aloud, "I'm a great boy, why this keeps happening to me?" He was little but he had a profound sense of cosmic injustice. He was a great boy, not just a good boy—a delightful self-assessment—how could life treat him so poorly? Shouldn't there be a connection? If you did everything right, shouldn't you be rewarded?

He remembers keenly all the injustices that ever befell him.

While he no longer expresses himself in precisely these words, he's wondering right now how he could be dealt such a blow. How could he possibly deserve this unfairness? I watch him cry, and we keep going.

Occasionally, but only very occasionally, we encounter someone coming down the hill, and we proceed on. We shoot for a curve in the road, and I'm hoping that beyond that we'll be close, but it doesn't look that way, no. We ask one of the descending pilgrims if we're close, and they say we're not, no. So we turn around and walk down. Still a beautiful walk even if we didn't reach our destination.

I will use this church in the future every time George misbehaves or doesn't eat the food that's put in front of him. I will point in the direction of the church and say, "*La chiesetta!*" And he will say, "No, *mamma*, no," but he will laugh, because in fact he won. Laugh, little boy, laugh, we will still get up there someday.

PISA

We go to Pisa. My uncle Nardo had shown me on a map where the tower is, it's across the river, the Arno. It looks very clear on the map, but when I get in the city, I get confused.

I stop the car next to two ladies who are chatting in the street and I ask them for directions, I ask for the square by name, Piazza dei Miracoli, Square of the Miracles. This is like asking for directions to the Empire State Building by asking the way to 34th and 5th, rather than just saying, "Where is the Empire State Building?"

They look at me kindly and ask, "*La torre?*" The tower? Duh. It turns out I was close. We park the car and walk.

Pisa is a sleepy little city, this is a hot summer afternoon when most people are staying cool indoors. When we get to the Piazza dei Miracoli though, it's full of people, people from all over the world. It's buzzing. It's not just the tower, there's a large white marble church and a baptistry, with a well maintained grassy area all around the buildings, and a clear sunny sky. It's white, green and light blue, and very bright.

There's a street on one side of the square where all the people are, with market stalls selling every possible knick knack, including miniature leaning towers of assorted sizes and Bart Simpson T-shirts. We walk onto the grass because there's no one on the grass, it feels nice to be away from the crowd. Then I realize there's no one on the grass because we're not allowed to be on it. We move back into the crowd before anyone chastises us, which would have happened.

Everyone is taking the picture of their friend propping up the tower, so I take one of George too. It's hard to get the shot because everyone is trying to get the same exact one, without everyone else in the shot. When I look at the picture later, he's sweaty and he's frowning. It's a good shot though, a classic.

We don't enter any of the buildings. There's an admission charge, understandably. It can't be easy to maintain this area with so many visitors. It's odd that there's a charge though because this is a church, people would need to be able to enter and pray. And in fact, there is a small side entrance for those who want to pray. This huge church built by people with huge devotion and huge fear of god—rich people but devout nonetheless—now exists for people—rich ones who can afford the vacation—who are devoted to their own entertainment.

We walk away from the tower and down a side street to see where my father went to college. On foot I have no trouble finding it. We are only a few blocks from the tower, but here there are few people, it's quiet.

My father attended the University of Pisa, which was founded in 1343, and where Galileo was a professor. My father had a special residential scholarship to the Scuola Normale Superiore di Pisa, a prestigious institution. My favorite poet, Carducci studied there as well. My father is very smart, he may be a downright genius. He studied aeronautical engineering in the 1950s.

The Scuola Normale is the bigger building in an irregularly shaped piazza, Piazza dei Cavalieri di Santo Stefano. The entire façade is decorated with black and white drawings, it's very unusual. There are steps going up to the front door, we go up the steps and look inside. For such a spectacular building, it has a small lobby, a bit institutional.

Also on this square was the tower where Conte Ugolino della Gherardesca was locked up and left to die with his sons and grandchildren. A plaque here commemorates the miserable event.

The story of Ugolino and his villain, the archbishop Ruggieri, is one of the most famous passages in Dante's Inferno.

Dante runs into Ugolino in the lowest circle of hell, gnawing on the back of the archbishop's head. They're both in hell together for eternity. Ugolino asks the visitor to let him tell his story, so that his words my bring infamy to the traitor whose head he is gnawing—so that he may add insult to injury. Dante is listening. At the end of his telling, Ugolino brings the entire city of Pisa into his vituperation, calling for a flood that will drown all its inhabitants. Here we are, 700 years later, in the city, on such a beautiful day.

~.~.~

On the way back to *la torre*, the tower, we pass a garage with this sign in English: Free to Leave the Transition. In other words, please don't block the exit, don't park here. It seems like it could mean so much more.

I always read into things, I see patterns and assign meaning to them, when they have no meaning. They just are. My second to last license plate in New Jersey, not a custom plate, just the next one on the pile, spelled out, with some creativity, "Why be safe?" My latest license plate spells out, without even much creativity required, "Late." I'm receiving a message via the State of New Jersey that I need to get out there, now!

SESTRIERE

Sestriere is all about the Olympics now. The downhill skiing events were held here in the Torino 2006 Winter Olympics and since then Sestriere is the center of Olympic everything.

It used to be an uncommonly unattractive ski resort, no quaint little alpine buildings but many large apartment buildings with tiny apartments. Sestriere was built in the 1930s. Whereas most ski resorts started out as the original alpine village nestled in the valley, Sestriere was built from scratch at the top of the world, with two distinctive round towers as its anchors. It's on a 2,000 meter pass, 6,000 feet up.

Sestriere may have been the site of Hannibal's crossing of the Alps with his elephants in Roman times. Some archaeological remains that may have confirmed the route were lost during World War II. No one knows for sure at what exact pass he crossed, and other passes are mentioned as well. Richard Miles writes about the crossing and says that Hannibal gave a speech to the troops once they got a broad view of Italy below them, and there is no such view in Sestriere. The broad view is towards France, the view towards Italy is blocked by mountains.

The town's official website covers the more recent history of Sestriere, in English: "The Commune of Sestriere has a very recent history since it was constituted ex-novo in 1934 with the name of Sestrières (then in 1935 lost the 'è' accented and the 's' final to the

French language following the dispositions of the regime becoming Sestriere) on the territorial district of the ex Commune of Champlas du Col , of the ex Commune of Sauze of Cesana and the fraction Village of Sestriere, detached it by the neighboring Commune of Pragelato. Subsequently, in 1947, it was again reconstituted the Commune Sauze of Cesana that went out definitely 'from the orbit' of Sestriere."

Like every place else in Italy, Sestriere has not changed, at least not very much. There is the new Olympic statue in the middle of the road that you have to drive around. There is the Olympic village they're trying to sell as condos. But there is still also the little gray church where we used to go to mass, standing room only during ski season. There's the movie theater next to the Galup bar and pastry shop. And there are still the mountains. Looking down towards France the view is long and spectacular. Looking up, there are the Banchetta, the Motta, the Rognosa, the Sises. They rise up to nearly 3,000 meters. It's summer so we're not here to ski but to hike.

You can't hike through the middle because there's a golf course on the lower ski slopes, the highest golf course in Europe, but it's easy enough to hike around it. Around it and up. There are well kept trails, and even off the trails, this alpine vegetation is very controlled. There are pine trees and grass and little flowers. It's not overwhelming deep woods that swallow you up, it's trees and grass and little flowers, and little streams. George loves the streams, and we stop at each one. The water is cold and clear and it makes a pleasant sound in the otherwise silent air.

I've skied here and I've hiked here. I know my way around these mountains. Because the woods are not deep, the town stays in view, it's easy to stay oriented. The lodges that cater to the skiers in winter are open for hikers in the summer. They have broad terraces in the sun that skiers sun themselves on, and they are wonderful in the cool summer air.

We hike up to the Chisonetto, an all-wood alpine lodge where I have a cappuccino and George has a hot chocolate. We used to stop here with my aunt to have a lunch break from skiing. We ate ham sandwiches and a light sweet wine called *frizzantino*. We drank the wine even though we were kids, just a small amount.

I have only one item on my bucket list, that I've shared with some friends, and that is to spend one winter skiing in Sestriere. The question is: Will I be unencumbered by employment before my knees give out? And if so, will I have the guts to just leave and come here to ski? I hope so. My sister, unlike me, always loathed skiing. If you look up "loathe" in the dictionary, there's a picture of her standing, on skis, waiting for the desire to move to come to her.

On the mountain across the way we see little gray specks that look like rocks but are in fact sheep. Someone is grazing his sheep, lots of them, on the summer ski slopes. George can't make them out, they're too small and they look too much like rocks from here. We will get confirmation tomorrow that these are not inert minerals but live creatures with active digestive systems—massive poopers!

We keep going. I remember that there's a dam up higher, with a lake. In fact, you can't see the lake from the ski slopes—at least not from the groomed trails—but I've hiked up to it a long time ago in the summer.

We meet a couple coming downhill and I ask them if there's a lake up ahead. One of them says yes, and the other says no. Huh? They tell me I'll see what they mean.

And I do when we get there. This is late summer and the lake is dry. George doesn't get why we came all the way up here. I try to explain to him, but all he sees is a dusty pit. A bit of a bummer. On the plus side, the rest of the trek is downhill.

After the nature hike we go into town. The shops are divided between those selling fine sportswear and accessories, and those selling toys and alpine souvenirs. George and I are both partial to the latter. There is no alpine souvenir I don't like, and George loves toys. He wants me to buy him a big Lego set. The perfect traveling toy, one with 400 little pieces... I don't buy it, and we don't buy any souvenirs either.

There's a festival in the center of town. There are booths selling handicrafts, honey, and salame. There's always salame.

We have pizza for dinner at a restaurant. A couple from England is sitting at the next table. I wonder if they would have thought of coming here before the Olympic notoriety. Other than this one time, most of our meals are at the Galup bar and pastry shop. They sell little rectangular *pizzette* that George likes.

We also go into the grocery store. This store was there way back when, same owners. The father is behind the deli counter, and the son, who is now middle aged, is at the register. They did move across the street. Like many Italian grocery stores, this store is relatively small but it sells everything, with one or two of each thing on display. These stores are a marvel to me, they're so neat and the food looks ... pretty. I get a cut of the local cheese, *toma*, and the father asks me if I want it *fresca* or *stagionata*—fresh or aged. I also buy honey for my aunt, who had asked me to get a particular kind.

The next morning we are up very early. We go to the Galup for breakfast and then head to a hike. Today we're going around the other side of the golf course. It's a beautiful sunny day, though a little cool. I only brought one sweater for each of us that we are wearing all the time. In all the pictures George is wearing the same thing.

We go by the Olympic village. It's a bit below the town, where the mountain starts to drop off towards France, so it's fairly unobtrusive even though it's quite large. A man standing in front asks me, "*Signora*, would you like to buy a condo?" I feel flattered, accosted on the street by a condo peddler. I must exude the aura of someone with the funds to buy a condo.

We keep walking with a view of the mountains towards France, the big open view. Some of the mountains have glaciers on them, I point them out to George. He's not terribly excited about this walk, and I'm not all that excited about it either. We're on a small road along the side of the mountain, we're not really hiking. So I decide to get off the road and go uphill, up the mountain, straight up. It's doable but it is pretty tough. George gets on one of his unstoppable tirades of complaining. He can't believe I'm making him do this, where are we going, why are we doing this, he wants to go back.

Pretty soon, as he sees that his speech is not working, he resorts to tears. He cries, and he's so cute when he cries. He doesn't think I know where I'm going, but I do. We're going to have lunch.

This lodge is on the Alpette, a shorter mountain right in front of the town. So we walked and walked and didn't really get very far. Mostly we moved upwards. It's decorated with traditional alpine décor, plus now Olympic memorabilia. The summer Olympics are on TV. I had never actually been to this lodge, it's quite large and very nice. As we wait for our lunch, sitting in the sun on the outdoor terrace, the owner brings me a slice of cured meat served on a piece of fried polenta as a complimentary appetizer. Lovely. This is followed by my lunch of polenta. Wonderful.

There are a few other diners, very few, relaxed, with children and dogs. In America, we would engage in conversation in this situation, a few travelers in an unusual venue, but here we do not.

After our meal, we leave in the opposite direction from which we came, and this takes us to where we saw the sheep yesterday. Underfoot we have confirmation that they were sheep—droppings everywhere.

Suddenly George announces, "*Cacca*!" It might be the big lunch, it might be the exercise, it might be the poop everywhere, it might be all of the above, but George has to go.

I tell him, "We'll get back soon. Can you hold it until then?"

"No, I have to go now."

"Well, we can go back to the restaurant."

"No, I have to go now."

"Okay, well, go here then." I figure there was so much poop up here already that his would not really make a difference.

He drops his shorts right there, squats, and makes a really big one, and then he wipes using leaves.

"Feel better?"

"Yup."

And we walk on, stepping carefully.

DRIVING CROSS-COUNTRY

We have to drive across Italy today. We have to. We need to get from Sestriere, on the French border, to Venice, where we have a hotel reservation for tonight. This is about the longest distance across Italy that one can go. It's 500 kilometers—300 miles. Mapquest gives it 5 hours and 2 minutes.

Calvin Trillin writes about Americans driving across the country as if they were being chased, always trying to cover more miles, not stopping. Maybe they need to do that, because their country is 3,000 miles across. I've personally done it, we stopped some, and it took two weeks.

But a certain faction of Italians, for all the slow life, loves to cover ground too, even if they don't have as much to cover. Or maybe because of it. You can actually get to your destination quickly if you step on it. In America you can't: you can get there from here, but not today. Italians give their travel times *da casello a casello*, from toll booth to toll booth, so they don't get penalized unfairly for the slow driving stretch getting to the *autostrada*.

I recall my uncle telling me once that someone passed him when he was driving 220 kilometers per hour. That's 130 miles per hour. It wasn't his own speed that amazed him. He was amazed that someone was driving faster.

But for every driver going breathtakingly fast, there's another one in a little car chugging along in the right lane. Not everyone drives fast.

When I told people I was going to Venice, every one of them asked if I was taking the train.

"No, I'm driving." It's 300 miles, for goodness sake, same as from my house to Boston or from my house to Pittsburgh, both of which drives I've done by myself—in bad weather.

We wake up very early in Sestriere because we have gone to bed early. Because there's no TV where we are staying. We go to breakfast at Galup one last time, and head down.

I call my aunt around 9 o'clock from an *autogrill* near Piacenza.

She asks, "Are you ready to leave?"

"Actually, we're in Piacenza."

"Already?"

"Yes." We're American. This is how we drive across the country: as if we're being chased.

VENEZIA

When John McPhee was a boy, he and his mother took multiple modes of transportation from New Jersey to LaGuardia airport to watch the planes land and take off. This was in the '40s, planes were a novelty.

George and I take multiple modes of transportation from New Jersey to Venice to watch the boats, a novelty for him. In a 1,000-year-old city, he is fascinated by boats.

It starts on arrival. We park the car and take the Venice equivalent of a bus, the *vaporetto*. We can go the fast way, via the Giudecca, or the scenic route, via the Canal Grande. The scenic route it is. The Canal Grande can only be traveled by boat. There is no sidewalk or boardwalk or quay that would allow you to walk along it. Venice is truly a city on water. And it's spectacular.

But first we have to find our hotel. I don't like to make hotel reservations because I can never find the hotel where I have the reservation, but I wasn't coming all the way to Venice not knowing if I had a place to stay. So I had made a reservation online, at a small B&B centrally located, in the San Marco district. I have the address, San Marco and a number. I believe this to be the name of the street and the number of the building. It turns out this is not how it works in Venice. This is a postal address: what I thought was the street is actually the neighborhood, and the number is a postal sequence number. Richard Paul Roe writes about Venice in Shakespeare's days, and he refers to the same problem, no street addresses then or now. He also quotes Venetian directions as written by Shakespeare: "Turn upon your right hand at the next turning, but at the next turning of all, on your left; marry, at the very next turning, turn of no hand; but turn down indirectly..." Even Shakespeare can't find the words.

So I booked my hotel online in America so I would have a place to stay, and now I can't find it. I know I'm in the right area, I'm right behind San Marco, but I don't know where the hotel is.

I'm carrying a duffel bag over my shoulder walking through very narrow, very crowded streets, only some three feet across, with people walking in both directions, holding George's hand. Normally in crowded circumstances I would make fun of the situation and say to George, "This would be the perfect place to lose you." And he would say, "No, mamma," and hold my hand more tightly. Normally I would scar him for life in this way, but not today.

I'm bumping people with my duffel, and I don't care. Ordinarily I would care and be careful of others. Someone yells at me, and I ignore him and keep moving. I step inside a lace store to ask them if they can point me to my B&B. They've never heard of it. George tells me, "It's okay, *mamma*." I'm near tears.

I pull out my phone and my hotel information and I call them up. I guess I could have done this already, but I did not expect this to be so hard. They answer the phone and very nicely explain to me how to get to them, I'm very close. A huge weight is off my shoulders. They are down one of the tiny three feet wide streets.

The hotel is above a restaurant. I have arrived at lunch time and the restaurant is full. I announce myself and they say, "We'll be right with you," very nicely. And then they keep me waiting. I go back and say I'd like to go upstairs. And they say, "Sure," and they keep me waiting. I am extremely aggravated. I know they take one look at me, an overwhelmed single woman with a ragged duffel on her shoulder, and they figure they can keep me waiting. By the by, a man shows us to our room, and he's nice, and he says they're busy because it's lunch time, and I'm still a bit cranky. The room is very nice, newly renovated with a great bathroom. The TV program selection is limited, a plus as far as I'm concerned.

We're in Venice!

~.~.~

We walk out to San Marco. The piazza is lovely, it's large with porticoes and pigeons, and the outdoor cafés, all with perfectly aligned chairs, each café with a different color chair. It's almost like any other nice city piazza, except for the huge ornate cathedral at one end. A combination of mundane and extravagant. The cathedral is elaborate with different color marbles and gold, and circular motifs and spikes. The decoration is not perfectly symmetrical. Next to it the Doge's palace is much more sedate, in a pink checkerboard lace.

We sit at an outdoor café. These are the famous cafés, I feel like a movie star from the 1960s. A waiter hands us menus and points out that there is a surcharge for the band. I'm so glad he pointed it out. I don't particularly like music and I don't particularly like parting with money, even for things I like, so George and I get up and go sit at the next café that has no band. George knows we're pulling a weird move, but he comes along. We can still hear the band, and pleasantly less loudly. I go back to feeling like a movie star. We have a beer and a coke, and they bring out a little bowl of chips. George is happy too.

~.~.~

Many years ago I came to Venice with my husband. It was winter, we were in Italy to ski and we made a side trip to Venice for a couple of days. We wore our ski coats around town, which an Italian would never do. They would wear a dark city coat, gray or brown, or maybe a dark green *loden* coat. In Piazza San Marco, an Italian said, looking at us and assuming I would not understand, "Why do they dress that way?" I was too mortified really to call him on it and let it go, though clearly I still remember. We tourists are expected to dress for the natives.

Back home one afternoon I was going down to Frenchtown for a walk and I was wearing a shirt with a hole on the shoulder. My mother said, "You can't go dressed like that, the tourists are there." We natives are expected to dress for the tourists.

~.~.~

Venice is a maze. There are a few principal thoroughfares that are marked, connecting the three main locales: San Marco, Accademia and Rialto. Everyplace else is a network of tiny streets that more often than not end at a canal. There are bridges with steps to cross the canals. There are only three large bridges that cross the Grand Canal. It's truly a city on water. It's a city of water.

Everyone knows about the gondolas but those are for the tourists. What's fascinating about Venice is that all the transportation of daily life is done by boat. In addition to the *vaporetti*, the buses, there are taxi boats, police boats, fire boats, ambulance boats, private boats, hotel shuttle boats, local government boats, lagoon environmental agency boats, delivery boats, boats with cranes on them.

As I point out the various types of boats to George, he gets more and more interested in the boat world. We sit on the side of the Canal Grande and watch the boats go by. He counts the number of different categories of boats that we are seeing. We do this for an hour at a time, at different spots. We have come to Venice to look at boats.

The streets around San Marco are crowded, filled with shops, both little local shops selling paper goods and masks as well as mall shops, designer shops. Some of the canals in this area have continuous gondola loops. If you get a gondola ride, you queue up behind all the other gondolas. We watch the gondolas go by, but we don't take a gondola ride. There's a stone sign: *Divieto di Sosta – Riservato alle Gondole*, Gondola parking only.

We discover hot dogs in Venice. They're called *wurstel* in Italian, and they are served cut in half lengthwise and toasted.

We walk across the Accademia bridge, and on that side of the Canal Grande it's quite a bit more quiet and a bit roomier. We walk to the back, to the Giudecca, the large deep water channel, we walk by the Guggenheim museum and we go to the big church at the tip, Santa Maria della Salute, which is round inside. This church was built following an outbreak of pestilence in the 1630s. When I will tell my aunt we went there she will say, "Oh, that church is new."

~.~.~

We get up early in the morning as we always do and go out. At this time of day, there's no one around, we have San Marco almost to ourselves. We go out to the Riva degli Schiavoni, we pass the Bridge of Sighs semi-enveloped in advertising. Like everywhere else in Italy these days, it seems, there are renovations. We find a local bar to grab *"un cappuccino e una brioche."* The barista is the owner, a middle aged woman who is clearly always here. We will return to the same place every morning we are in Venice, always early in the morning.

The tour groups start to arrive, hordes of people get off various boats led by their tour guides holding a recognizable gee-gaw up in the air.

Occasionally while we're in Venice, we will see a cruise ship go by, through the Giudecca, taller and bigger than Venice itself, outsized and out of place and time. The city that ruled the sea, is now overshadowed by a single ship.

I'm walking on a bridge, the bridges have long steps, I'm looking up at the scenery at the same time, and I trip on one of the steps. I hold tight to my camera because I don't want it to break even though ironically the lens will jam shortly and I will not be able to take any more pictures for the rest of the trip. I hold on to my camera and I go flying. I put two large gashes in my leg where my leg hits the step, I'm very hurt, my leg hurts. I'm klutzy and have fallen before, but this is a lot of hurt. Not one person stops to help me.

Thankfully I have George with me, who is such a kind little boy, and he is very supportive, "Are you okay, *mamma*?" I'm okay but I cry a little bit, maybe more because now I have an excuse to release some pressure. The whole trip has been pretty stressful, traveling to different places with a small child, I feel so responsible for him and for our safety every minute of every day. We sit on a bench and use some water to wash the wound.

When I will return to my aunt's house, she will bandage my leg. In fact, she will bandage it hugely, with big pieces of gauze attached with medical tape. I will make fun of the bandage, the wounds are deep but not wide, and the second bandaging she will do will be more moderate. I walk around with a big thing attached to my leg.

~.~.~

On our way out of Venice, we take the *vaporetto* back to the car. A young man accosts us and strikes up a conversation, he's trying to sell a little ribbon bracelet, he's a runaway maybe, and he goes on and on, and I really don't want to deal with him. I tell him I'm not interested, but he keeps going, he keeps talking to us. Finally I do give him a euro and then I rudely tell him to leave us alone, which he finally does. I am a very polite person, I have a hard time being flat out rude, and I resent that he puts me in a position where I have to be. When he gets off, before we do, he makes a point of saying good bye. That also aggravates me.

This is our last taste of Venice, our last opportunity to look at the city from the Grand Canal, I really am not happy about wasting these last few moments on this guy, imposing his runaway poverty on me.

BARDOLINO

On the return from Venice I want to stop off at one of the lakes, Lago di Garda. It seems it's on the way though it's not really. Everything looks close on a map, and I get fooled every time.

We get off the highway and along the way enter one of the many tiny rotaries. They're really just a regular intersection with a little round space in the middle and rotary signage. This one is confusing and we go round and round until I decide on a direction which turns out to be the good one.

We stop at the town of Bardolino, a supremely well-ordered town, cheerful but not too much. I am not a big fan of the lakes, they're pretty but I have yet to understand them. They're pretty. So?

Lago di Garda in particular has significance for me. This is where my husband proposed. Not in Bardolino, but just south of it. We stayed at a hotel called Regina Adelaide, in the winter time, it was quiet, and in one of their salons he proposed. He had brought the ring all the way from America, it was a big deal, and it was cool. I tell George about this, though it doesn't grab him.

At the end of our last trip with George, on the way to the airport in Milan, we stopped at Lago Maggiore. It was a weekday, I was told that it was because it was a weekday that it was deserted. We had an ice cream cone and left. So, I don't really get the lakes.

Bardolino is pretty, we walk along the lake, we have an ice cream cone as usual, we buy my aunt some wine. It's difficult to buy my aunt food and wine because she's so particular about what she eats and drinks, so I don't try particularly hard, I buy some *bardolino*, because that's where we are. Then we leave. Lots of driving still to be done to get back to Liguria.

ARIANNA AND HER DAUGHTER

Arianna is coming to my aunt's for an afternoon visit, with her daughter Francesca. Arianna is in her late 80s, she's widowed, and Francesca is divorced, so they live together in a beautiful family home in Savona. On the phone they tell me they would have us over but the house is being cleaned and the drapes are down. I would not care really. In fact, I would like to see the house, I would even like a complete tour of it, which I've never had, I've only ever seen the living areas.

Arianna is thin and well-tailored, she is as always dressed perfectly: skirt, jacket, pumps with heels. She's doesn't look her age at all. She has a lovely smile and she says gracious things. But she doesn't remember anything.

She compliments George, what an attractive and nice boy he is. She seems to know who we are, or is she just saying the right things for the occasion, by rote? I have read that people lose first what they acquired last, so they don't recall what they did yesterday, but they retain longer what they learned first, a sort of last in first out inventory, so they remember things from long ago, including the basics one learns as a child, basic social skills, what to say in what occasion. Is she being kind because she's known to say the right things all her life?

Arianna is technically my grandmother's first cousin, though she was born 20 years after my grandmother. Arianna's mother was my grandmother's best friend, and my aunt is named after her. Both of Arianna's parents died when she was still a child, and she went to live with her grandmother. Eventually her grandmother died too, and my grandmother took her in. So she spent her later youth as my mother's and my aunt's older sister.

We have black-and-white pictures of the three girls looking cheerful and pretty.

They lived through difficult times together, during World War II.

My grandfather was a naval office, a career officer. His own father was in the Finanza, the financial police, and he died young. My grandfather's sister Marta, who was the baby of the family, remembers riding in a carriage after he died, a rare event. She thought it was exciting and didn't understand why everyone else was crying. Because of this military connection, my grandfather was able to go to the Naval Academy, something he wouldn't have been able to do otherwise. He was tall and handsome and he looked good in his uniform. He was also kind and gentlemanly, and poor. My grandmother came from a well-off family, her own parents died young. She was not well educated but she was a sharp dresser—she bought her clothes in Genova.

They don't seem like a good match but they were married for over 50 years and always appeared very devoted to each other.

When war broke out, my grandfather was in it even though he was in his 40s, because he was already in the Navy, he was a naval officer. There were times when my grandmother did not know where he was at all. She had three young girls in her charge and not much of her money left.

Midway through the war, Italy switched sides. The figurehead king signed an armistice with the Americans and pulled out of the alliance with Germany. And all hell broke loose. As the Americans moved up the boot from Sicily, the Germans moved down from the north. All young men were at risk. If they had been fascists, they were targeted by the anti-fascists; while the resistance fighters were targeted by the Germans. And everyone was one or the other. You couldn't claim you were just a bystander. Many people were shot.

My grandfather got lucky at this point, as lucky as you could be in a very difficult situation: he was not on a ship. He was, family history tells, second-in-command at the naval base in La Spezia. He was on land, he was able to escape. And escape he did with the whole family, my grandmother, my mother, my aunt, and Arianna.

They spent the rest of the war in a small village under the Matterhorn, or the Cervino as the Italians call it, the village of Valtournenche. My grandfather passed himself off as a math teacher. He was a little older than a regular soldier, so it was plausible that he may not have been involved in the war. There were food shortages of all kinds, and they had their own cow.

There are several family stories from this time. One was that my aunt and Arianna were walking in the mountains above the town and they ran into German soldiers. The soldiers asked them what they were doing and they said they were picking flowers, and the soldiers left them alone.

Another time German soldiers came into their house and searched it, looking for who knows what. What they found to their liking was a leather jacket, they tossed it out the window to pick it up on their way out. Arianna, who had been out at that time, returned home, saw the jacket outside, wondered what it was doing there, and picked it up and brought it back in. So the soldiers never did take it.

There was a group of Jewish friends in the town, also escaped from somewhere. They are known by my mother as *gli ebrei di Valtournenche*, the Jews of Valtournenche. She still mentions them at times. They had a German shepherd. They listened to Radio Londra, that transmitted messages in code. They left when the Germans arrived, on foot over the mountains to Switzerland, and left the dog with my mother's family, as well as some papers that my grandmother destroyed. My mother ran into them in Torino years later, so thankfully they survived.

~.~.~

Arianna's daughter has had cancer. She's in remission and doing apparently well, but she will die soon after. I will never see her again. And Arianna too I doubt I will ever see.

ALARM

In the house, suddenly, a horrible clanging very loud noise starts, and keeps going. I don't know what is going on, but my aunt does: George set off the burglar alarm. She fumbles around to turn it off and then immediately calls the Carabinieri to tell them that it's a false alarm and that they don't need to come.

An hour or so later they show up anyway. They said they want to make sure we're not held hostage, but they don't seem too worried. We exchange pleasantries and apologize, *"Sa', il bambino…"*

FAREWELL DINNER

My cousin Nino comes to dinner with his family at the end of our stay with his wife Linda and their son who is four years older than George and very, very tall.

They just got back from a vacation in the South Pacific, a two-day flight from Genova through Germany and Los Angeles, a once-in-a-lifetime trip.

On the way there they went to the Grand Canyon. I ask them if they had taken the mule ride into the canyon and they hadn't, they had been on a helicopter ride. They also stopped in Las Vegas, and they ask me about it. What's the deal with Las Vegas? I tell them I personally do not see the attraction, I have been there for work and would not ever consider going for fun. I like nature and quiet and old places, pretty much the un-Vegas. They were a little mystified by it too.

On my work trip, we stayed at the Venetian, and one of my co-workers told me that he imagined that this is what Italy looked like. A Las Vegas casino? No!

They ask me if Americans eat fruit, that they didn't see fruit served in restaurants. I tell them that grocery stores sell fruit, and that restaurants sometimes serve berries, *frutti di bosco*. They are a little doubtful, they imagine that even if there is fruit in America, surely it must not taste good. I tell them that where I live we have farm stands. "*Ah, che bello.*"

One time an American woman told me that all Italians want to move to America. That's not really the case at all. America is a source of curiosity and fascination, and it's a great place to visit, but Italians feel a little sorry for us.

MILANO

We are back in Milan on our way to the airport. We are here because George recalls the trams with such fondness, so we are back to see them.

As usual, finding downtown Milan by car is a major chore for me, somewhat stressful. I do find it, we park right by the Castello Sforzesco, a prime tram location. It turns out George does not find them as fascinating now as he did last time. The novelty is gone, they're ho hum. I am kind of mad about it, because we could have gone somewhere easier to get to that we had not seen before, someplace truly novel.

He's mildly apologetic, but basically his premise is that he can't help it if they don't interest him anymore. He's still completely genuine, no guile, which is endearing, and I get over it.

We go through the park, the Parco Sempione. This is where we came every day when I was really little, before I went to school. We rode our bikes and roller skated. It's a big park, with lawns and a lake, and roads, and big century-old horse chestnut trees. Very stately, as befits Milan. We walk to the other end, to Piazza Sempione, with the *Arco della Pace*, the arch of peace, a grandiose Roman-style arch with horses on the top. We used to live right off this Piazza, and we go look at our old building. It doesn't look like much, but it's nice to see. The apartment had a big terrace all along the front of the building, and a smaller terrace along most of the back. The building is set back from the street, it's a newer building, with a small garden between it and the street. George has very mild interest.

To kill time, I decide to go see Leonardo's Last Supper. I wish to see it only really to kill time, but this is absolutely one of Milan's finest gems. And in fact, there's a wait. I ask how long the wait is, thinking we can walk around a little more and come back, and the cashier says, flatly, "Two weeks." Oh well, we will have to kill time some other way, on our way to the airport and then home.

NEW YORK CITY

We leave the house at 9 a.m. which beats all the traffic on a Sunday. No one is driving around at that time—except my friend Bob, I see his car driving through town.

George reads. "*Mamma*, guess what? The Hardys are going to Princeton."

"What for?"

"For a case."

The plan is to drive up the west side of Manhattan, park there, walk across the park to two museums that have special exhibits.

It takes a while to get uptown, and after some circling we come upon a parking space on 88th Street. A little close to a hydrant, but not too close. I'm very pleased, and then as we walk towards the park we come across another parking space, and then more parking spaces—there's a veritable abundance of parking spaces on 88th Street.

We emerge from 88th Street onto Central Park West and at the first bench George says,

"Can we sit down?"

"No."

We walk through the park along the reservoir, which is officially called, according to a plaque, the Jacqueline Kennedy Onassis Reservoir. She lived on upper 5th Avenue, right by the reservoir. There are signs indicating that walking and running should be done in a counterclockwise direction—the path is small—and that dogs, bicycles and strollers are not permitted. Walking through the park is a bit disconcerting because the paths curve, so it's hard to keep to your aim. I keep my bearings by the buildings on Central Park West and 5th Avenue, but I always feel like I'm swooshing in different directions, and then I don't know where the park gates are—where's the nearest gate, where will it place me?

Somewhere along the way George eagle eyes a pretzel vendor and gets a pretzel. The vendor asks me if I want salt and I can't understand him. I make him repeat it more than once and finally George says, "Salt, *mamma*. He's asking if we want salt." I feel inept at pretzel procurement, a skill I thought I commanded.

We come out of the park on 5th Avenue a bit below the Guggenheim and we head higher to 92nd and 5th, to the Jewish Museum that's hosting the Curious George exhibit.

I did not know the story of A.H. Rey and his wife Margret who narrowly escaped the Nazis leaving Paris for Lisbon on bicycles with their drawings. They switched to trains and boats and ended up in Brazil and then in New York City. Their story shows up in the Curious George stories in various themes. The exhibit is lovely, there are both great drawings as well as documentation of their ordeal. They come across as very positive people who even as they fled for their lives continued to produce beautiful drawings and worked to get them published.

There's a small room arranged with pillows and many Curious George books, including some in Hebrew and some in Spanish. On the ceiling of this room there is a mobile of Curious George drawings of fish, and there's a dock with feet dangling from it on the ceiling. The effect is that you're underwater in a Curious George picture.

George says he's going to read all the books. He sits down with a stack of them and starts. I should be overjoyed that my son wants to read all the books, that he's a reader, what mother doesn't want her children to read, I should be so proud and supportive. Oy vey. I suggest that we may not be able to read them all here now today. We came to New York today and we have to get our New York's worth, he can read the books at the library. He says he's going to read them all. "Look, *mamma*, this is the first one." It's the one where the man with the yellow hat takes George home for the first time. Some of the original drawings from this book are in the exhibit, I explain that they are the actual drawings, that they're not a page from a book. He says, "I get it!" I tell him I will be looking around the exhibit.

A man is showing his son the blurb on a book jacket, and I tell him I have to see it too now, I'm curious. He says this is the only children's book jacket he's ever seen that refers to Hitler. It talks about how the book almost didn't make it out to be known. I tell him I didn't know the story of the author and he says his children did a project on it at school. He is a really nice man with a number of children who are running around, and he talks to them very reasonably, doesn't lose his temper. The children seem to be both overwhelmed and underwhelmed by the exhibit.

George comes looking for me. "I'm still here," I tell him. "You won't be able to read all the books." He goes back to them.

There is a collection of new year's cards drawn by A.H. Rey. From them I learn that the couple lived at 82 Washington Place, off Washington Square, and at 42 Washington Square, on the square itself, and also at 14 Hilliard Street, in Cambridge, Massachusetts.

I finally pry George away.

Of course he wants to go to the gift shop. He knows I won't want to buy anything and it's his little game I think, to see if he can wrangle a purchase. None of the Curious George merchandise interests him. He would like a Noah's ark toy. "No." Then he sees a "One Fish, Two Fish, Red Fish, Blue Fish" in Hebrew and he thinks it's wonderful. Because he knows the books, he feels that he's reading Hebrew. He's pleased with himself. I'm *ferklempt*, he's such a reader, he is.

~.~.~

On the way down 5th Avenue we make a stop at the Cooper-Hewitt, which is a Smithsonian museum. It's not, however and disappointingly, free. Since we don't really have time to spend today, we only look around the lobby and, on George's insistence, the gift shop. The building is an old mansion, and the lobby is spectacular. It's wood paneled, with a grand wooden staircase. The gift shop is also a beautiful room, with a smaller room to the side. Both look out to the garden.

In the shop, George finds a picture book about the three little pigs with an architectural theme, and he shows me one of the house drawings and he tells me he thinks it's beautiful.

"It's Fallingwater, that's Fallingwater. It's a Frank Lloyd Wright house. Did you know that? Does it look familiar? It's a super famous house in Pennsylvania."

He says no.

Note to self, Go to Fallingwater sometime.

We don't buy anything.

On the way down 5th Avenue again, we stop at the Church of Heavenly Rest, and remarkably this church has a café annex with red tables and chairs outside on 5th Avenue. The café is called the Heavenly Rest Stop and its logo is a red coffee cup and saucer with a halo. I am pretty sure this is the first time I've been to a church café. They have salads and sandwiches and pastries and also beer and wine. I'm only guessing but maybe because they're a church they have special liquor laws? Or did they get a liquor license?

~.~.~

Back on the move, to the Metropolitan Museum of Art. The building is huge, with enormous columns on the front. There's a short line to get tickets. A French family cuts the line and I don't say anything at first and then it's too late to bring it up. And although they get tickets ahead of us they are dithering in the lobby and then get turned away by a guard for having a large backpack that they will need to check, so we still win.

George sees a small sign about an exhibit of King Tut's tomb, and he wants to go see it and we head there first. We do and I thought it was very cool but he did not find it very exciting. It's not the gold and the glamour of the boy king, it's the mundane part, the cloth used to wrap the mummies, the sawdust used to fill in the bodies where needed, the flower and leaf and bead necklaces they were buried with. Even though the leaves and flowers and dessicated, they can tell what plants they were, and, based on the flowers, in which month King Tut died. Amazing, it seems to me.

Next we head to the Picasso exhibit which is very crowded and very large. At the entrance there are some photos of him wearing shorts and no shirt, and he's quite muscular—an old-fashioned stud.

There are very many art works in several rooms, organized by type of work—each room is a different style: the blue period, the rose period, the Cubist period which unexpectedly for me is not the majority of the work, then portraits and drawings. He was phenomenally prolific, he did so many pieces.

There is a bronze sculpture of a woman's head, Cubist in style, all jagged instead of rounded. It's just like one we saw somewhere in Washington but we can't remember where in Washington.

We then go to a European painting section with many, many famous paintings: Monets, Van Goghs, Cezannes.

George asks of a garden bridge by Monet, "Are there many of these?" He's trying to figure out if the museums pass the same painting around among themselves. He's thinking: Why do I see the same thing?

There's a self-portrait of Van Gogh, and I point out we had seen one in Washington. George points out to me the differences between the two. He's way ahead of me.

There are seats in the center of each room, very little seating in relation to the number of visitors. The seats are piled with people facing different directions, each trying to get a little bit of seat for himself or herself. It's exhausting.

I tell him, "He did different versions of his paintings in different lights. In fact there is a set of three paintings of the Tuileries, at different times of day in different seasons. They are clearly all of the same subject, though the point of view is slightly different in each one.

We find ourselves in a sculpture gallery with many Rodin sculptures, including a small Thinker. This is our third Thinker. This sculpture is part of an enormous doorway.

There's also Adam, all ashamed.

George asks, "Where's Eve?"

"Right over here. They're both always made to look ashamed, with their eyes downcast and using their arms and hands to cover their naked bodies."

"What is the story of Adam and Eve?"

So I tell him, and he says, "Isn't the serpent the devil?"

"I guess so. Is that how you heard it?"

"Yes." So he knows the story, he's just checking the facts.

There's a sculpture of a painter who made a painting that's exhibited across from his bust.

There's a Balzac, our second Balzac.

There's the hand of God holding two people in it.

There are numerous studies.

The Met is such a maze. Even with the map it's hard to figure out. I ask a highbrow lady behind a little counter the way to the courtyard. She says, "The European sculpture courtyard?"

"Yes, the one with the benches." The one with the benches, and maybe there will be some art there too, that would be fine.

When we get there, there's another Rodin scuplture, the Burghers of Calais. They're an unhappy bunch. We sit on a bench next to them.

A guy tries to exit the museum via the emergency exit and the door doesn't open for him. He's wearing a striped shirt and around his waist a striped sweater with a different color combination.

We see a statue that I think is of St. George slaying the dragon but it turns out it's St. Michael slaying some scaly creature.

"*Mamma*, did dragons exist?"

"No, they really didn't."

"But dinosaurs really existed and they don't anymore, so why couldn't dragons exist?"

"No one has ever found evidence of dragons' existence. But they have found evidence of the dinosaurs—lots of it."

"So who did the knights fight?"

"Each other."

"WHY??"

There is an exhibit of Italian renaissance drawings, very pretty single color drawings, black and white or brown and white, with elaborate shadings so they're in fact really vibrant. They are a family's collection, the Tobey Collection. In the same room, there are cartoon drawings of semi-vintage but definitely recent-century New Yorker cartoons about museums. I'm mystified by that and find out later in a New York Times article that the cartoons were drawn by Mr. Tobey's father. Mystery solved but still a bit odd. Usually I come across the same thing in very different settings, but here I find two very different things in the same setting.

We stop by the shop to buy a gift that I want to bring to Olivia in Italy. To get to the scarves we have to walk through the toys, and George finds the Lego sets. These are architectural models made out of Legos—including one of Fallingwater. We do not buy any. I do buy a very nice silk scarf, made in Italy, to bring as a gift to Italy. It would have been more environmentally sound if I had just bought it there rather than sending it twice across the ocean. George picks out the color, a nice pink and lavender with leafy swirls.

~.~.~

I have been reading a book by Adam Gopnik called Through the Children's Gate where he opens by explaining that Central Park's entrances have names, and the one at 76th Street and 5th Avenue is called the Children's Gate. On the book jacket there's a picture of it. I had shown the book to George before we left the house and told him we were going to see it. The name of the gate was behind a hot dog vendor, carved in the stone like on the book jacket. George was a little disappointed that there isn't an actual gate, just an opening in the wall with a path leading into the park.

We exit the park via the Mariners' Gate.

George asks, "What's a mariner?"

SAG HARBOR

I am so excited, we're going to Sag Harbor. This is where John Steinbeck had a house, and he left from this house for this Travels with Charley trip, the name format I used for this book. I will be able to see the house.

We go over the Verrazzano Bridge to go to Sag Harbor. Verrazzano is spelled with two r's and two z's in Italian but the bridge signs usually have one z. It's a most spectacular bridge. Lore has it that the engineers had to take into account the curvature of the earth when they built it—because it's so long. From up top there's a spectacular view of New York Harbor.

"George, look up from your book and down at the view."

"I'm reading."

"But look, there's a great view from up here."

"Okay, I looked."

When he's not complaining, he's indifferent, reading the Hardy Boys.

There's a little map of Long Island in the big road atlas. It's hard to get lost going to Sag Harbor because you basically just keep going and then turn left. In fact, that's how an Italian would give you directions, "Go out Sunrise Highway and before you get to the end, turn left." But I'm still referring to the map.

"Look George, this is JFK, the airport the Hardys left from when they went to England."

"Really?"

"It used to be called Idlewild."

"Okay."

I pull over at one point to consult my map. Long Island has great place names, I read them off, "Massapequa, Islip, Patchogue, Bayport..."

"Bayport?"

"Yes, Bayport."

"There's a real place called Bayport? Show it to me on the map."

"Okay, why?"

"That's where the Hardys live!" Steinbeck and the Hardys in one trip, what a literary excursion.

We stop in Southampton. Many of the stores are jewelry stores. This really is a ritzy place. George sees a foam sword that he would like, but we don't buy it.

There's a pretty museum called the Parrish. On the building is a depiction of St. George slaying the dragon. On the side of the museum, in an enclosed grassy area, there are multiple busts of Roman emperors arrayed in two rows facing each other, with a full statue at the far end. This is not what I'm expecting to find at this sandy vacation spot, though perhaps it speaks to the modern masters of the universe that reside here. We look at each one, they have the name of the emperor under each one, and there are two of Julius Caesar. On the side of each one, it says that it was made in Florence.

On our way back to the car we plan to stop at a nice coffee/bakery. George trips and falls and slightly hurts his left elbow—I say slightly because it wasn't bleeding, but he put as much drama into the situation as he could, holding it and looking as concerned as he can look, which is not very. Then we walk into the coffee/bakery and one of the workers has his left elbow all bandaged up. I ask him what happened and he tells us he fell off a motorcycle. I tell him my son just tripped on the sidewalk and hurt his elbow. He's sympathetic, though even George at this point has a hard time holding on to the drama. It's slipping away from him and, as he would say, there's nothing he can do about it. The young man tells me, "Don't let your son ride a motorcycle." I assure him I will do everything possible so that he doesn't.

We are done with Southampton and move on to Water Mill. There is not much in Water Mill other than the water mill. We are meeting my friend from Brazil and her daughter who are coming by Jitney, the bus from Manhanttan. By this point we have had many exchanges with them changing the meeting time and place as the day unfolds. The latest is we will meet them in Water Mill. She wants me to ask where the bus stops. I tell her it's a tiny place and she will see the mill, we will be at the mill. We sit on a bench near the water mill for a while, George reads, the Hardys get into scrapes, he rests his head on me, we have a nice relaxing time.

One Jitney goes by and doesn't stop. A few moments of panic ensue. A second Jitney goes by and stops. We run to meet my friend and her beautiful daughter who had specifically requested to see Easthampton, the glamour of which is evidently lapping at the Brazilian shores. I assure her there's nothing to see in Water Mill and we move on to Bridgehampton and then Easthampton. Fancy shops and fancy cars abound. We see several Ferraris, a Lamborghini and a Maserati, all in quick succession. We pick up real estate flyers that offer multi-million dollar houses for sale. Rentals go for multiple thousands of dollars per week.

"How do so many people have this much money?" I ask. "I can see how some people have this much money, but how can so many have so much? What do they all do?"

"I don't know," my friend says.

She buys George an ice cream while I'm not looking and later she will tell me she thought I was mad about that. Not at all, he loves ice cream, she gave him some joy.

~.~.~

Sag Harbor is the residence of one of my college friends and this is a get together with a bunch of them coming from Brazil, New Jersey and Massachusetts. George loves hanging out with this crew.

The next morning's plan is to go out on my friend's boat. Boating looks relaxing and peaceful but it's actually difficult and stressful. Thankfully I'm a tag alonger at all boating events and have to be concerned only minimally, and primarily with hanging on to something.

First of all, we need to prepare to go boating. This includes assembling lunch, need to have lunch. The hostess insists we take the leftover fried chicken from the night before, so we do. We also bring some fruit, crackers, peanuts and brownies. To drink we have water and *limonata* S. Pellegrino—unbeknownst to anyone this is a treat for me, reminds me of my childhood, etc.

We also need towels, life jackets for the children and *schmutz*—code word for sun block. We don't bring enough food, but we bring many towels, thankfully as we will find out, and lots of *schmutz*, both spray and spreadable.

George says, "I don't know what's going on."

I tell him, "Don't worry, honey, I don't either." This answer completely satisfies him, I think this displays the confidence of a child in his parents. If you don't know what's going on and that's ok, then it must be ok.

Second, we go to the boat. We drive to the marina in multiple cars and find a place to park. Today is farmer's market day so the parking is extra specially limited. Then we have to take the dinghy out to the boat, and the dinghy's engine won't work—technically the issue is with the contraption that's supposed to supply fuel to the engine from a plastic canister. I'm extra special glad I'm only a tag alonger. Half the crew get on the dinghy and row out to the boat. George and I are part of the second half, so we wait on the dock watching the dinghy boat away.

George says, "I don't know what's going on."

He sees one little boat, he is assuming that that's our day trip, and he's looking for a second little boat for the rest of us. I understand the source of his confusion and I explain to him that the little boat takes us out to the actual boat that's going to hold all of us.

"Ooooooh." Finally there's some clarity, though he does ask, "Why don't they pull the boat up to the dock?"

"I don't know. It's not correct boating procedure. I don't know."

We wait a while and the dinghy comes back, with the motor running. Someone figured out that if the plastic canister is held over one's head, the fuel will flow to the engine. Bonus!

Finally, we boat. We all get on the boat and after assorted trafficking of ropes and cushions and the like, we leave the harbor under power. Even though it's a sailboat, we are motoring. Soon it starts to rain. Then it starts to rain harder. Then it rains in chunky drops that hurt when they strike you. I am glad to put a towel around me. Then it thunders and lightnings and we turn the boat around and head in.

When I ask George later about his favorite part of the trip he says, "The boat ride."

"But it rained."

"That was the best part!"

I realize on the drive home that I completely forgot to go see Steinbeck's house. I contact my friend who contacts his friend who knows everything and I'm able to see it via Google maps.

TRIP IV: NOVELTY

"Ti canteremo noi cipressi i cori
Che vanno eterni fra la terra e il cielo."
                    Giosue' Carducci

We will sing you, we cypress, the choruses
Than go eternally from earth to sky.

DECISIONS

"Do you want to go to Italy this year, George?"

"Fine."

"Really?"

"Yes." In an eye rolling kind of tone, without the actual eye roll, eye roll implied. Like, really, okay, I will subject myself to that.

"What would you like to see in Italy?"

"The Colosseum."

"That's not near *zia*'s house, is there anything else you'd like to see?"

"No, just the Colosseum."

"Do you think that someday you would like to see the Great Wall in China?"

"No."

"Just the Colosseum?"

"Yup."

LUCETO

On the way back from Sassello I have passed the sign for Luceto every time and not taken the turn. Today I turn. I haven't been to Luceto in over 20 years. I think it's 100 yards or so after the turn, but it's not quite that close. I keep going, and I don't recognize any of it, I'm not sure I'll find it. Then suddenly, maybe a kilometer from the turn, not far after all, I see it. It looks nothing like I remembered it, but I know I'm there. There's the little square to the right off the main road where you have to leave the car because the streets are too narrow for cars. There's the little church with the little steeple that has been restored and repainted into a little bijou.

To the extent that every village has its church and every church has its village, Luceto is a tiny village with a tiny church. It's on flat ground near the river, or rather near the dry river bed.

We leave the car and walk. The street runs between walls, with *orti*, vegetable gardens, not visible on the other side of the walls. We turn right under the little arch where the swallows had their nests. We keep walking, with the walls now gone and the *orti* visible—little plots of land meticulously tended.

We walk by a group of people sitting and chatting, and we exchange a "*Buona sera.*"

Then we get to the house. This house belonged to my grandmother's family. During the war, World War II, my mother lived in this house. Savona was being bombed, so my grandmother and her brother took their families here, for safety. Her brother had a bomb shelter built into the hillside behind the house. I remember seeing the small cave.

My grandfather was a career officer in the navy, so he was in the war immediately. My mother remembers hearing the declaration of war on the radio, and she remembers them being sad because they knew her father was going to be in right away.

My mother remembers multiple families living in the house together during the war, different families coming and going at different times. It's a nice house but not huge: two stories, three windows across the front, two across the side.

For many years the house was in *usufrutto*—available for use—to a broad number of descendants, but when my grandmother's generation passed away the house reverted fully to one set of heirs who live in Uruguay. They sold it.

There were caretakers, permanent residents of the house. They were there during the war and forever thereafter. I remember them both. They were a married couple, Pedrin and Carmela. Pedrin's regular job was at the port, where he worked as a longshoreman. In the evening he would come home and take his *caprette*, his goats, to the dry river bed where they would graze. My aunt remembers that he had more than one goat, while my mother remembers him having only one, so there's a discrepancy in the historical record.

He would come home at the end of the day and ask Carmela, "What's for dinner?"

"Potatoes and beans."

"Again?"

I don't remember the goats, but I remember him: he was strong and very tanned, and he wore a dark blue sleeveless undershirt. He rolled his own cigarettes, which I had never seen anyone else do.

Carmela was small and also very tanned, and when I knew her she wore her gray hair in a bun. My mother remembers her going up the hill behind the house, known as Garbugia', to collect herbs. I remember arriving at the house once to find her sitting up straight on a little stone bench that was attached to the side of the house, in the sun, immobile, like an old Italian woman Buddha. She had lived here for so long, she must have sat on that bench so many times. Was she thinking, or just sitting? I wonder.

Back to the present, George and I walk up to the house and there is a dog, a German shepherd, that barks at us furiously and continuously from behind a fence that surrounds the garden. I see the steps leading up to the house, I see the top of the gazebo, I see the house, but I don't get to enjoy it. I remember next to the steps, there was a tree with a bed of lilies-of-the-valley under it. I would like to see if it's still there, but I can't. I planted lilies-of-the-valley under a tree in my garden in New Jersey because of this tree in Luceto.

On the way back, we stop at a little grocery store, one of these small stores that sell two of everything, and I buy some *aranciata* S. Pellegrino. The owner is speaking dialect to the customer before me, then he switches to Italian to speak to me. He gives George a piece of candy even though he knows I'm not a local, he knows it because he's not speaking dialect to me, and even though he must suspect he'll never see me again, he does this small kindness.

I tell my aunt later that I went to Luceto, and she says they repainted the house but not well. I tell her I think they did a pretty nice job, that they painted Art Nouveau accents, what the Italians call *stile* Liberty, around the top, which would be appropriate to the age of the house. She's not entirely convinced that I know what I'm talking about, but she concedes that if they did, that's good.

SAVONA

Savona could have been Genova if not for the events of 1528. That year Genova dumped dirt and debris in Savona's harbor, *l'interramento del porto*, and Savona was forever after relegated to a minor city.

The rivalry between the two cities goes back much earlier than that, it goes back 2,000 years—that we know of. During the Punic Wars, Savona sided with Carthage against Rome, Genova's ally, and we all know how that war ended. Savona did not pick the winner.

Genova called itself La Superba, while Savona had no proud moniker. But Savona does have a claim to fame that it doesn't necessarily flaunt: it is the hometown of two popes. Not any two popes, but two Renaissance popes. And not any two Renaissance popes, but none other than Sisto IV and Giulio II, uncle and nephew from the same family, the Della Rovere.

Sisto IV commissioned his namesake chapel in the Vatican, the Cappella Sistina, and Giulio II commissioned Michelangelo to paint the ceiling. So they were big. Very big. If they were Genoese everyone would know, everyone knows Columbus was Genoese, but Savona plays it cool with its super popes.

~.~.~

Today we are going to Savona with my aunt to settle a dispute.

One of my aunt's oldest friends has told her in a recent phone call that Savona is ugly. This pissed her off, and we're out to prove that Savona is in fact excellent.

We go to the Via Pia, the oldest part of town, a narrow pedestrian street. All the buildings along the street have stone bas reliefs above the doorways, and those are the only true ornamentation on the buildings. The Ligurians are known for their frugality, and Ligurian buildings' decoration is entirely painted on. Cheaper than carving stone.

Over the years the paint has faded, and only recently the buildings all over Liguria are being repainted. The ones along the Via Pia are beautifully done, all of them. They've all been redone with exquisitely detailed painted cornices, window ledges and the like.

Today is a sidewalk sale day on the Via Pia. The street is very narrow and it doesn't have sidewalks, so the sale items are in the street and it's very crowded. We're walking slowly three across, blocking the flow of people. George is clinging to me until I get exasperated and yell at him, "Stop it!" A few heads turn, then turn away. I'm kind of embarrassed. I can't understand his perspective right then, but later I will realize he's a little guy in a little crowded place where he doesn't speak the language. If he loses me, he will be completely helpless. He's going to cling to me as if his life depends on it, which it does.

We get to a wider part of the street, a very small square, where there are two marble plaques on the side of the building commemorating the native popes.

As we keep walking down the street, the crowds thin and we advance more pleasantly. We turn right, and after a few more turns we get to the cathedral.

Next to the cathedral is the Sistine chapel. Not the one in Rome obviously. Savona has its own Sistine chapel! All the times I've come here, I did not know that. And it's open to visitors today. We walk inside, there's a docent who can answer questions. I tend to avoid helpful guides, I can't think of intelligent questions, I'm afraid I will get stuck listening to answer much longer than my attention span, I don't want to bother them, I don't want to draw attention to myself.

My aunt, on the other hand, is very gregarious, not at all shy, and quite pleased with having family visiting from America. And she opens with, "This is my niece, she's visiting from America."

The man was very nice, he told us a lot about the chapel. It was a Renaissance chapel, later redone so it's all flowery. It's very pretty, quite a treasure.

We finish the outing sitting at an outdoor café, reviewing our evidence. We conclude definitively that Savona is excellent.

BIRTHDAY PARTY

We have been invited to a birthday party by my mother's cousin Ginevra. It's the birthday of George's friend Baldo, a friend from prior visits. I tell George he's super lucky to have a friend in Italy and to be invited to a party. He does think it's pretty cool. I buy two little toy helicopters for him, only to realize he's now 15—much more grown up than I remembered him. I apologize to everyone for the ridiculous gift, and of course everyone is gracious.

I have never been to Ginevra's house so I need directions. I am to turn right into her road and go uphill, and then, "When you get to a little wall, call me." I don't see a singular little wall that distinguishes itself among all the other little walls, and of course this is a little tiny road, with no room to pull over anywhere. I find a little place to stop down a little side street, and I call her.

She asks, "Where are you?"

"I am on a little side street."

"Where is that?" She has no idea and I have no idea.

After some back and forth she tells me she's sending someone out for me. Sure enough, here is my mother's friend Olivia greeting me. I was right there. There's actually a little parking area at her building, and it's among olive trees.

She had said it would be a *merenda*, a snack. When we get there she has a wonderful buffet, much more than a *merenda*. She has prosciutto and salame and figs, salad, a ham and potato tart, pizza, and other goodies.

The kids go upstairs and after a little while George comes back down and sits and sulks a bit. I ask him why he's not with the other kids and he says they're watching volleyball on television. I try to tell him he has to go hang out with them even if he's bored, that he's being unreasonable and unpleasant. He won't budge. Soon enough Ginevra asks me why he's not hanging out with the other kids and I tell her the truth—I probably should have lied, but I can't think of a plausible lie right then. I try to be offhand and humorous about it, because really he's being difficult and that's his problem rather than everyone else's. But she does what I knew she would do, she immediately heads upstairs to tell the other kids they need to entertain George. She puts the onus on them to be polite to him when he's the one who's being rude to them. This is the extreme politeness of Italians, it's part of the social fabric.

She shows me her garden and her house, I've never been there before. This is her summer place, twenty minutes away from her main home. Her garden is on multiple levels, there's a patio, a lower lawn area, and a still lower area with trees that leads out to the street. There are olive trees in her garden.

The apartment is on three levels: there is a living room on the lower level, another living room upstairs, and then her bedroom on the top floor. From the bedroom window she has a great view of the mountains and the sea. It's a very cheerful place.

She shows me large landscape paintings that she has all over and tells me that her husband painted them. He passed away, and she tells me it was 18 years ago. Such a long time. The paintings are nice, I don't recall that he painted. He was a fun person, they never had kids and they had fun together, and I think she misses him every single day.

Her niece arrives. Although she's my second cousin I have only seen her just a few times in my life, but I do recall her as very nice, and she is in fact chatty as well as very well dressed in a modern and pretty outfit. She lives in Milan, is married with no kids. She keeps a sailboat in Savona. We chat and take each other's pictures, all the niceties.

Ginevra tells the story about me that she always tells. One time I was in Milan, and she and her husband took me out to dinner and then drove me back home, where I was staying. When I got out of the car, I took off my shoes right on the sidewalk. My feet must have hurt quite a bit. And they thought that was absolutely a fantastical thing to do. I still remember the outfit and the shoes I was wearing that day.

I tell her that I have recently run into some people she knows. At a high school reunion of my American high school in Italy, held in San Francisco, I ran into three sisters who lived in the same building in Milan as Ginevra, back when she lived in Milan. I bring greetings from them and their mother, and she remembers them well and gets goose bumps. She tells me she had taken English lessons from their mother, who had told her, "I'm very proud of you." She says the phrase to me in English, and I tell her she says it really well, and she's pleased and laughs. These things don't just happen every day.

The birthday boy is Filipino and his whole family lives in the area and is attending the party. They are cheerful and fun. Instead of pointing to George as the rude boy, as they should, they are enthralled with his blue-eyed looks and tell each other and then me that he looks like a movie star. I'm not sure about the looks, but he certainly has a prima donna attitude on display today.

As the party winds down, the kids are back upstairs, this time playing video games, and I have to drag George away.

LUNCH WITH CARLO

We have a lunch guest at my aunt's today, Carlo. I have met him before, on an earlier trip, and I look forward to seeing him.

His significance is this—and it's from another world: he is my uncle's friend from prison camp. They were imprisoned together in Germany in World War II. Thankfully they both returned, and while my uncle has passed away, Carlo has reached the age of 87, he is a widower, and he is here having lunch with us.

When I will tell my parents I had lunch with him, they will say, "Oh, yes, that's your uncle's friend from prison camp." Of course. Everyone has one.

Interestingly, as an engineer, he also knows my father and his brother professionally, completely unrelated to this other family connection.

We eat outside. He is a lovely man, very proper and thoughtful. We talk about Obama, about Carlo's new car, about my own rental car which I scraped this morning in the parking garage at the Coop. I show him my rental contract to get his opinion on whether I will get hit with any repair costs. He assesses, accurately as it will turn out, that I will not have to pay any damages.

We talk about his family and how busy they are, we talk about his summer home here in Liguria—his full time home is in Milan. He wonders if his children will take care of the house when he's gone, something my aunt also worries about—grown children they all are.

My aunt wants to leave the house to her sons in the best possible shape. She contrasts that with other people she knows who plan to leave all the repairs to their heirs. There is no right answer, I don't think.

We talk about his grandson, an engineering student, and about the new specialties that exist in engineering, and how the kid likes theoretical studies.

My aunt suspects that Carlo would like to be a matchmaker between his grandson and her granddaughter, but if he does, he's very subtle.

FIRENZE

The travel writing industry does not give due justice to the travel part of traveling. The travel part of traveling, the getting there, is hard. I think it's because travel writers love to travel so much that they bear that part.

I have quite a concern about being able to find the hotel in Florence, navigating the city by car. On the other hand, if I take the train it will take longer and I won't then have the flexibility to do a little side touring and visits on the return. I have to drive there. I have Mapquest directions from the *autostrada* to the hotel in about 30 different turns. Plus I have an accordion map I have put together by taping together Google maps. I am well armed but still wary.

We get off the highway in Florence at a huge toll booth. I ask for some directions from the toll booth operator. I then stop to get gas. I don't know how to pump gas in my rental car. I can't even get the tank open. I approach an attendant even though I'm technically at the self-serve pump.

"*Per cortesia*, can you help me? This is a rental car and I don't know how to pump my own gas."

"No problem, *signora*. This is how we keep our jobs." He's grateful and pleasant. I ask for and receive some more guidance to get to the *centro*.

I let George know that I will be stressed for a while now, he's forewarned.

I make two wrong turns but recover and make good progress until, very close to the hotel, there's a detour. I try and I try but I cannot recover from it. I cannot make my way back where I want to be. Too many one way streets. I see a sign for a parking garage and I go for it. We will have to abandon our car.

We emerge from the underground parking garage and I don't know where I am, I'm all turned around, and I don't know which way I'm facing.

I approach a woman who's at her car and I ask her, *"Per cortesia,* I'm trying to get to the cathedral. Which way is that?" I expect her to just point in the general direction. Instead she gives me precise instructions, and then repeats them. "Make a right over there, make a left, go by the *poste nuove,* the new Post Office, and keep going straight." I laugh to myself because the *poste nuove* in Italy could well be 400 years old, but these are not, they're very 20th century.

Once I start walking I turn around and try to get my bearings. I want to make sure I can find my car again. She approaches me again to find out if I am confused about the directions. I explain that I want to make sure I recall where I left the car. She tells me, "This is the Sant'Ambrogio market." What I will find out later about the Florentines is that they're all very proud of their city. They are not curt to the tourists, they are gracious and kind and pretty funny too.

After settling into the hotel, we leave it looking for a place to eat. We are starving! We stop at pretty much the first place we find, with no discretion or discrimination, other than it happens to be on the cathedral square, across the street from one of the most famous, most elaborate, most beautiful churches in the world. Other than that, it's no big deal, just the first place we found. It's a cafeteria-style place, I select a *prosciutto crudo* sandwich for myself and George goes for the pesto ravioli. We sit at a little table and eat with gusto. George will remember this little tourist trap fondly, as something wonderful about Florence, in spite of all the true world wonders across the street.

After our late lunch we start walking around. We walk past the church to the Piazza della Signoria. Here is yet another of the most famous vistas in the world. I try to explain to George that he needs to soak it all in. He wants to but he can't put it in context.

He tells me, "I don't know what this is. Why is this important?" It's great that he senses this is supposed to be great, and that he wants to know.

I explain the Renaissance to him: first there were the Greeks and the Romans, then there were the Dark Ages when all that classical knowledge was set aside, and then the Renaissance brought it back, all the knowledge and splendor that the new riches of the time could buy.

We walk up to the Palazzo Vecchio. We walk in the small courtyard. We walk into the next courtyard. It seems we can visit the building. I have heard that it's difficult to get into the museums, that you need reservations or stand in long lines, so I'm not sure if we can get in.

I walk up to the ticket booth and ask the man, "Can we get tickets or are there lines? I heard there are lines."

He replies, "*Signora*, you are the line."

"Oh good. It's me and the little boy."

We complete the transaction, and he says, "Now, there is no line!"

Funny guy. One thing I will notice throughout is that Italians are comfortable in their jobs. They don't leave their personalities at the door and acquire their work persona. They are who they are all the time.

The Palazzo Vecchio is super fabulous. There is a huge Sala dei 500 with frescoes on the walls. George is not completely engaged.

We pass a statue of two men engaged in wrestling. One is being held upside down by the other and retaliating by grabbing the first figure's penis. There are two French women looking at the statue as we walk by and I point out to George the penis squeeze. I say it in English but the two women understand and smile. George is kind of embarrassed.

I tell him, "George, it's funny."

"It's not funny." Okay.

I wish I knew more about history, there is so much to know.

I show George the six balls of the Medici shield and tell him he will see those all over Florence, he can look for them—kind of like looking for Waldo.

We enter the Penelope room. I know this story. I tell it to George. She weaved during the day and undid the work at night, waiting for Ulysses to come back, so she wouldn't have to marry any of her new suitors. It's one of those funny stories that are clever but odd—no one noticed that in ten years she made no progress?

There's a small room that no one is going into. It contains the—the—portrait of Machiavelli. I just read a book about Machiavelli, and this is the—the—portrait of Machiavelli that was reproduced in the book. Oh my goodness. The. Portrait.

Outside of Palazzo Vecchio and in the Loggia dei Lanzi are various statues, the most famous of which is Michelangelo's David. Even though this might be the most famous statue in the world, I have never really gotten that statue. David was the underdog. Why did Michelangelo make him huge and powerful?

For all the beauty, Renaissance Italy was, I believe, a cruel place. I love reading history but I struggle with the cruelty. Savonarola was burned to death right here, in this magnificent square. Modern times are less violent, it's empirically true, yet even in modern times cruelty and suffering affect so many people. What made me live in peace and safety rather than elsewhere or at another time? I am bothered by that question.

As a woman in Renaissance Italy, I would have been a mother or a nun. Dava Sobel writes about Galileo's daughter, from a privileged family, who was fortunate to be a nun. And she was content, she was a positive person, and she wrote to her father and took care of things he needed while she was hungry and cold in her convent. Her sister, also a nun, was much less happy with her situation. Both of them had no control over their lives at all.

Piazza della Signoria is a pedestrian zone, there is a very visible police presence, the city police. They wear big white tall helmets, very architectural and authoritative headgear. And they stroll in pairs, they stroll leisurely, more leisurely than the tourists, and they chat. They are engaged in a conversation that has nothing to do with policing, I can tell that by their expressions and their movements.

A German car has accidentally driven into the Piazza and stopped. The people in the car realize they shouldn't be here, though they don't seem to know what to do about it. They are looking around, and looking up at the buildings, as in, "Wow, look where we ended up—right in the middle of everything." The police have not accosted them yet, there's no urgency, they're in the wrong place, it happens. We move on before resolution.

~.~.~

The next day we have a big day planned. Or rather, I have a big day planned, and George is going to hate it. We're going to walk all over the hill on the other side of the Arno.

We make our way over and chance on the entrance to the Giardino Bardini. We walk in and the lady at the counter explains that with the one ticket we can see the Giardino Bardini as well as the Giardino di Boboli as well as 3 other small museums. And George gets in for free—so it won't cost him anything to hate it. Hate is free.

She explains to me how to go from the Giardino Bardini to that of di Boboli. I don't understand the first time and she explains it again. She must do this many times a day, yet she is very polite and pleasant. She hasn't left her personality at the door, she's talking to me like a real person to a real person.

The Giardino Bardini is absolutely lovely. There is a formal garden on a steep hill, then a pergola, then an olive garden, then a loggia. From the loggia we can see Florence from above. What a view. There are small tables and chairs in the loggia and we sit down. It's early but presently a small café opens up in a small doorway at the far end. I walk over to see what they have and order a glass of water and a cappuccino. The young lady brings it to us on a little tray. She seems to be very relaxed in her work, and has an ongoing conversation with another Giardino worker. I'm thinking they work together every single day, yet they seem to have a lot to talk about.

After the loggia we go through a wooded area, past the greenhouses, we find the dragon stream, and then go by the villa. We leave the Giardino and find the way to the Boboli exactly as explained.

At the Boboli entrance, at a back gate, there are two ladies at the ticket booth, also engaged in an involved conversation. Once again, I think they work together every day and spend the day chatting amiably with brief breaks to sell tickets. I ask for a map of the Giardino and she says sure, and hands me one.

The Giardino di Boboli is huge. Huge. It's more huge than beautiful. We walk from one end all the way to the other. At the other end there's a fountain with an island. The fountain is so big that it has an island.

We leave the Giardino from a side entrance looking for some lunch. We end up on a little street and stop at a little bar that has a few sandwiches in a vitrine. I get a *prosciutto crudo* sandwich, and it's truly the best *prosciutto crudo* sandwich I've ever had. The *prosciutto* is delicious and sweet, which it's supposed to be, it's not supposed to be really salty, and there's a lot of it. We sit on a stoop and eat our lunch.

We walk down, down, down a very steep hill. To our left are the old walls of Florence and in the little green strip between the walls and the road are olive trees.

At the bottom, in a small doorway there's a small little shop, maybe 4 feet by 4 feet. Inside, an Asian woman is painting little watercolors of Florence and displaying them for sale. They are lovely and only 2 or 3 euros for little tiny ones. I am enthralled but keep going, though I will buy a little watercolor on the way back. George will choose a panorama with the cathedral in the center, exactly what we've been looking at all day from the hill facing the city.

We head uphill again, towards Piazzale Michelangelo and San Miniato. The way up is on a steep pedestrian street. There is a cross, and another cross, it's a Via Crucis. This hillside road reminding us of the suffering of the Christ leads to a big tourist bus parking lot with great views of the city.

~.~.~

We go to breakfast in the hotel in the morning. Breakfast is in a narrow room with a long counter on which is laid out a luscious display including a coffee cake and Nutella. Plus cereal and yogurt—healthy foods if healthy foods are desired. I go for the cake and George discovers Nutella. And loves it. He spreads it on little slices of bread, many little slices.

Breakfast is hosted by a Florentine woman who likes to engage in conversation with her guests and proffer advice on all topics. This is a fairly common Italian attitude: since they've been doing everything the same way forever, they are very clear about how everything should be done, and they will tell you.

There is an American couple sitting at the counter with us. The Florentine hostess doesn't speak English, so she engages with them in Italian, which they don't understand. She keeps going and I feel obliged to step in to translate, which I hate doing. I don't want to get involved, and invariably we will come to an odd word that I can't translate, and everyone will look at me as in, "You don't know? How do you not know? Maybe your Italian (or English) is not that good after all." To which I want to scream, "Hey, you only speak one language!" This always happens, I end up the dog.

This couple had been to Fiesole, a nearby town, and the woman has a pain in her foot. The hostess provides medical advice as well as directions to the nearest pharmacy.

Then, her duty done with them, she turns to us and asks us what our plans are for the day. I tell her we are planning on visiting some museums. She advises us to go to a medieval armor museum that's world class and located in a villa. It sounds interesting until she tells us we have to get there by bus. I don't think so. We are in easy walking distance to some of the world's most fabulous things to see,

I'm not spending time on a bus. Public transportation is great but it takes time.

I kind of skirt the bus issue and tell her I would like to see some of the museums in town, but that I'm afraid I will have had to have reservations. She says that's just for the Uffizi, and that the hotel could have gotten me a reservation with some advance notice. I had tried online but the site didn't work. She recommends the Bargello, and I will take her up on that.

I pry George away from the counter in a Nutella stupor. When we return home he will find out that the local IGA carries Nutella and will say, "Why haven't you ever bought any?" So now I do. Because I too love Nutella. So we can get stupefied right at home.

We leave the hotel for our day of museums, and head for the Bargello. It's located behind Palazzo Vecchio. While it's not as well-known as the Uffizi, its collection is considered very important. There are guards at the door, it's quite early, we're almost the only visitors. They let us in cheerfully. The building was the city's courthouse and prison in the Renaissance. The guards explain to me that when its bell tolled it was always bad news. You were lucky if it didn't toll for thee.

At the ticket booth, the clerk asks me if I'm Italian. I say that I am, and she asks me for my documents. I guess my crystalline accent is not enough. I babble that I don't have them with me, which is true, I left them in the hotel, and she looks at me like I'm a liar and a cheat. Evidently there's a reduced admission fee for Italians or maybe for Europeans, but I didn't ask for the reduced rate, she offered it! I tell her I'll pay the regular rate, which turns out to be a few euros, not very much.

The building has a courtyard encircled with arches of perfect semi-circles, with a giant staircase at one side. The salons around the courtyard contain a fabulous assortment of treasures, from famous Donatellos in the Donatello room, to a bust of Michelangelo, to Renaissance pottery and jewelry, lots of it. George is intrigued by some of it—typically if he has a frame of reference, he's heard of Michelangelo for example—and bored by some of it. If they ever made a movie and called it "Night at the Museum: Battle of the Bargello," children all over the world would know their Donatellos like they know their Easter Island heads.

There's a David by Donatello that I think captures the sense of David as a small fellow facing Goliath, David is youthful and slim, very different from Michelangelo's. And the sculpture is life size rather than gigantic. There's a Cupid by Donatello that looks like a cheerful and chubby kid. There's a St. John the Baptist who looks like he hasn't eaten in a month, very gaunt. There's also a St. George with a giant shield. He looks strong and dignified. I like Donatello.

After the Bargello we stop at a fancy bar for a cappuccino and something for George, and then fortified we head to the museum of the history of science, now called the Galileo museum. This is a low-key museum from the outside, behind the Uffizi. I have to ask to make sure I am headed in the right direction. Once inside though, the lobby is modern and bright, and the admission fee is relatively high. This museum has been renovated with apparently a big budget. It's the nicest I've seen in Italy in terms of displays. The artifacts are arranged by topic in individual rooms, and each one has its name tag, plus there are videos to explain the science. We go to the restroom, and that is brand new too.

Science aside, the items themselves are beautiful works of craftsmanship. Each scientific instrument back then was made by hand, with lots of wood and brass parts. There is equipment by Galileo, plus a piece of his finger: even in science the tradition of reliquary persists.

George gets bored after a while, and I get bored a bit too. I don't know much about science, so I can appreciate the form of the pieces but not so much the function. I do feel though that we visited a very special place, this is a very special place with very special pieces. Beyond the arts, the Medici also patronized science. Plus they were what would now be called hoarders, they were avid collectors, and they had the money to buy the best of everything. Money in itself is nothing, but here in Florence you can see that money well spent moved the world forward at the time and transmitted the learning and the pieces themselves to us. It's pretty cool.

Now we are hungry and we head to one of the feed-the-tourists shops along the main tourist drag. I get a *prosciutto* sandwich and George gets a fried chicken sandwich. We sit in the back of the store, at an outdoor table. The whole setup is pretty bland, with aggressive pigeons too, but George declares his sandwich the best chicken he has ever eaten. I'm glad his grandmother is not a witness, she would be plunged into deep despair to hear such a thing.

We stop in the hotel for a brief respite, a chance to rest our feet, then we're off again. There is only a small Italian-only TV, so I don't have to fight that battle constantly.

We head back out, this time behind the hotel. The Accademia that houses the real David is here, but we don't go in, we keep going to another selection of museums back here.

The San Marco museum is closed, it just closed for the day. We missed it. It houses the frescoes by Beato Angelico, one of the monks living in what was a monastery. He painted little frescoes all over the place, in every room practically. You can imagine the conversation at mealtimes, "Whatcha working on, Angelico?"

"Oh, I'm doing a little Coronation of the Virgin in Fra' Girolamo's cell."

"Ah, sounds inspired."

Only we can't imagine it because we missed it.

We go to the archaeological museum. This museum is the complete opposite of the science museum, in subject matter and style both. The museum is undergoing renovation, and it doesn't seem to be very far along. There's no sense of: Please pardon our appearance while we renovate. Rather it's: Good luck finding the galleries. We cross a large open space and go upstairs on makeshift stairs made of scaffolding materials. We get to the galleries, and they are ancient. Every place in Florence is ancient, but this place looks like the home of your weird old aunt who keeps all the knick knacks she has ever gotten and doesn't believe in dusting. It could use a renovation, though it has a certain charm that goes with the artifacts.

There is vitrine after vitrine of small Etruscan statues. Every maybe twentieth one has a little label typewritten on a typewriter. Occasionally there's a sign indicating that a statuette is missing, on loan to an exhibit in Berlin or Massa Marittima. Without the sign you'd never know it wasn't there, there's a clutter of figurines.

There are employees of the museum engaged in the usual daylong personal conversation. I ask if I can take pictures and they say yes, but no flash.

Subsequent rooms have Egyptian treasures. This is the Etruscan and Egyptian show-off-all-you-have museum.

Next we go to the Spedale degli Innocenti. This is located on one side of a square surrounded by loggias with again the perfect semicircular arches. The building's loggia was designed by Brunelleschi and it is famously decorated with round ceramic bas reliefs by the Andrea Della Robbia depicting swaddled babies. This was an orphanage, an organization that took in foundlings.

We go inside, and inside too there is a courtyard with the perfect semi-circles, and then another courtyard. This is a very plain place, a little sad but also hopeful. A Unicef organization is housed here, and there is also a museum. We walk through the courtyards and up a nice stairwell to get to the museum. Considering we're in Florence this is an odd museum. We are handed a little booklet that we can study while we are there to understand the collection. We have to return the booklet when we leave, so it's nice that they care about your visit, about maximizing your understanding of it.

And the items on display, considering we're in Florence where everything is super famous, are not things I recognize. So far today we've seen a slew of Donatellos and Galileo's finger, now we're looking at assorted paintings seemingly unconnected to each other except for the fact that they're in the same room. In fact, there's a significance to the collection, some of which has been sold. There's a painting of a Madonna surrounded by swaddled babies with the loggia of the building in the background.

One thing that is unique and very interesting is a collection of items that the foundlings had with them when they were left at the hospital. Looking at these, I get a sense of the heartbreak a mother would have felt leaving her child.

Back to the Cathedral, there is no line to go inside the church, and so we do. It's very simple inside, in contrast to the extremely elaborate exterior. On the way out again, we pass the entrance to the campanile and I ask George if he wants to walk up to the top. He says, "No." No hesitation, no doubt. I'm too tired myself.

We then visit the museum of the Duomo, which is behind the cathedral. This is quite nice, it's in an old building with a renovated interior. The guard lets George in for free and instructs him to walk underneath the turnstile. I wonder if this is a trick, can this be the official way to enter? And George is a little nervous, he's very compliant, but we do as told and sirens do not go off and we are not embarrassed. That's the risk we faced, embarrassment, which is the worst risk.

This museum holds many of the more important artifacts from the church, for safe keeping. There are also models of the church and some of the tools that would have been used at the time for construction. The church is most famous for its cupola, designed by Brunelleschi in a feat of extreme engineering for the time.

What's also here is a Pieta' by Michelangelo. There's an explanation that the figure standing at the back representing Nicodemus is a self-portait. This is our second Pieta', so it's kind of a cool find.

We came to this major center of art, Florence, and we hit all the minor museums. We did not go to the Uffizi, the Pitti, or the Accademia. I feel that we've seen a lot though, and we save the rest for next time, there can well be a next time for Florence.

After some additional rest in the hotel we head out to the market at San Lorenzo, just a couple of blocks away. The market consists of a very large number of stands selling primarily leather goods. My mother told me to make sure I buy a gift for my sister, and I'm looking for one. I think a purse of some kind would be useful and appreciated. After going back and forth some, I settle on a booth that has small roundish long strapped bags—in very many different colors. So I spend a lot of time trying to pick the perfect color. I end up with brown. Yes, brown. The seller is Brazilian, she came all the way from Brazil to sell bags at the market at San Lorenzo. Or maybe she came for something else and ended up selling bags at San Lorenzo.

The church of San Lorenzo has an unfinished façade—a view of what is under the beautiful marbles. Beside the church are the Medici tombs sculpted by Michelangelo, but we don't go in. Something else we will not visit, we'll have to come back.

It's evening now and we walk aimlessly until we arrive to the river, the Arno, near the Ponte Vecchio. We settle in at one of the bridges over the river. Where we are standing there are cars coming from the street along the river turning onto the bridge, and cars arriving perpendicular to the river to go over the bridge. The two flows of traffic are merging onto the bridge, the ones coming alongside the river have a yield sign, the others have a traffic light a block away. The traffic is active, it looks chaotic but as is often the case in Italy, it works. We stop and watch it. This is what George loves to do, to watch traffic, he's delighted by it. And we have found a great spot. We hang out for a long time, as the sun gets lower and the buildings become more golden than they normally are.

George's favorite vehicle in Italy, bar none, is the three-wheeler cross between a motorcycle and a truck that is used for small and cheap transports. He thinks it's the greatest.

I have to balance actually seeing some of the sights we came to see with doing what George likes to do. We have to do both: we have to see the sights but I can indulge him too. It's easy to make him do things, he can't help it, but he's such a nice child that I enjoy seeing him have fun. And he will remember the trip in its entirety more favorably if he has these wins, these highlights that are his own.

ROMA

We have reservations for the bullet train, the super high speed train, the Frecciarossa—Firenze Campo di Marte to Roma Termini in an hour and a half, at speeds of some 200 miles per hour. We are going to see the Colosseum.

The train is at 9:30 in the morning. We will walk to the station. We will walk even though the lady at the hotel said to take a taxi. We will walk because I'm crazy, but we will walk, and we do walk, and we get there very much ahead of time. In spite of two stops for assorted breakfast pastries and drinks. So we sit in the station and we wait. Waiting is not what George does best, he fidgets.

Campo di Marte is not Florence's main station. The main station is Santa Maria Novella, next to the church of that name. That's a head-in station. Because the high speed train is looking to get through quickly, it uses Campo di Marte which is a through station. It's a quiet little sleepy station.

I'm not sure what to expect as far as how long the train will stop. This is a high speed train, it cannot stop for very long I don't think. Though it does. It stops with plenty of time for us to find our carriage and our seats. But I don't know that at the time, so I run, and I make George run. The seats are not numbered exactly sequentially like one would expect. I can't imagine why. We do find seats next to each other that are not exactly our reserved seats that were not next to each other. We sit next to each other and there's a little table in front of us and two seats across the table. An older lady is sitting across the table. Her traveling companion, a man, is not sitting with her.

A group of three ladies going to Rome on a vacation rearrange themselves from their own separate assigned seats to the seats across the aisle from us. They talk the whole entire time. They are nice but quite boring, though clearly they enjoy each other's company. They have a Michelin guide to Rome that they are consulting. I'm not used to seeing Italians with guides, more so the non-Italians.

By the by, the ladies across the aisle pull out little snacks, and so does the lady across from us. On the way back we will find out again that everyone brings little snacks, little cookies, little sandwiches, little juice drinks. George asks, "Why don't we have snacks?" We are not following proper high speed train protocol or absorbing the full experience that would involve eating a snack.

From the train station, the Colosseum is not far, so—map in hand—we walk down some streets, by a church, through a park. As we get to the end of the park, there are tour buses parked along the curb, we must be near something touristy.

We see a piece of a large gray building behind some trees, and I'm not completely sure, but I do believe that's it! That's it!

"George, look, that's it, that's the Colosseum!"

We rush to get past the trees to see it better. And it is, it is the Colosseum. It's right in front of us, and it's huge, and it looks like it's supposed to look.

George says, "I was going to try to be cool about it, but actually I'm really excited."

We walk down to it, and then we're not sure what to do. Is there an entrance? Where is the entrance? We find the exit and we're told the entrance is on the opposite side. It's really big to walk around, and it's really hot and sunny.

We find the entrance and there is an enormous line.

"George, do you want to go inside?"

"Yes."

"Are you sure?"

"Yes."

"Because this is the line, it's really long. And four across."

"I want to go inside."

"Okay."

I have to agree with him, we need to go inside. Normally with a long line I would say, we'll do it next time, but there is no next time here, we have to go inside today.

We stand in line with many other people. It's hot. The line is disciplined. It's a bit wide, some four people across, but it's disciplined

Next to us there's an odd couple, an older American man and a lovely younger Filipino woman. They are clearly a couple, but a couple with friction. He is boastful and she's resentful.

He boasts, "You can ask me for anything. You asked me to buy you the fan you're holding."

"I bought the fan I'm holding, you wouldn't buy it for me."

"But you were free to ask me for it."

How not to win an argument with a woman.

A Colosseum worker comes alongside the line and explains in English, Italian and French that there is a guided tour available in each of the languages. The cost is 4 euros per person and if you are interested you can exit the line and follow him. Can this be for real? Only a few people are taking him up on it.

I ask him, "How long will this line take?"

"About a half hour."

"I would like the guided tour."

We exit the line and follow him loosely to another line. I'm very confused, I'm not sure which other line we should be in. I feel that George will feel my stress and go into panic mode. I'm trying to be calm. Somehow I end up in what I think is the correct line.

The American with the Filipino woman are now next to us in line. He's also confused and stressed. He's asking for further information. The 4 euros for the guided tour are in addition to the admission fee of 12 euros. He's disputing this with the Colosseum worker, who is engaged in discussions with him, the worker is staying with the man even though he really could ignore him. I wonder at that, what makes this Colosseum worker who works in this absolute chaos of an environment stay engaged when this man is arguing with him—unreasonably at that.

The worker argues cogently, "Why would you think that a guided tour would cost 8 euros less than general admission?" Is this man trying to impress his woman?

We finally get to the window and buy our admissions. It turns out George gets in for free, which I didn't expect, so instead of paying 24 euros for the two of us in the long line, we pay 12 euros for me and 4 euros each for the tour, a total of 20 euros. I jump the line and save 4 euros!

I ask the ticket agent, "Do I have to wait for the tour?" This is the last hurdle, the tour doesn't start for another half hour.

"*Signora*, once you're inside you can move about as you please."

Success! Though we should really take the tour and learn all kinds of things, we don't.

We put our tickets through a turnstile and enter. It is still enormously confusing. We manage to go right and into the arena area. We walk a bit. But what we would like to do is go upstairs. How do we get upstairs? We go back the way we came and I'm terrified that we will accidentally exit and have to go through the line again. That is my fear at that moment. We make our way around the Colosseum and finally get to stairs to go up.

There is an exhibit of artifacts found in the Colosseum over the years. Among them are animal bones, a bear skull being the most interesting specimen. There are other exhibits of replicas of gladiator outfits, many of them. They're pretty cool.

"Why did the Romans have brushes on their helmets?"

"I don't know, honey."

We wander some more and then George is done. We find our way back downstairs following some people down some stairs labeled "Emergency only." George knows we're being illegal and starts to point it out to me but then wisely keeps silent and follows me down the stairs.

We then have to make our way all the way around and across to the other side for the exit.

Outside, there are a couple of souvenir stands and one single food stand. George wants to buy something to eat. The single food stand is sitting on the sweltering asphalt outside the Colosseum, there is no place to sit. I tell George, "Let's go somewhere else, somewhere in the shade."

He's furious with me, he wants something now, but I move on.

We go by an arch and then have two false starts trying to walk through some of the adjoining ruins. We have to turn back, the areas are fenced off. This is very aggravating. The place is huge, and we're being corralled so we can't just walk. We end up having to walk down the avenue, the Via dei Fori Imperiali, beautiful name, nasty walk. Crowded. Very sunny and hot. No respite from the heat, no shade. We do buy some water.

Around the Colosseum there are people dressed in gladiator outfits that pose for pictures. We do not indulge but it's fun and funny.

Halfway up the Via dei Fori Imperiali there's a little visitor center. We go in, and there's a snack stand—possibly the most pitiful snack stand in all of Italy, though there is some shade and there are some chairs. George wants to eat here. I tell him, "George, this is the most pathetic snack stand in all of Italy."

He doesn't see it at all, but I'm the one who has a hissy fit now, and he backs off.

Inside the little visitor center building there is a model of the forums as they used to be, and he likes that. I don't really know what a forum is. I will have to research that.

We keep moving. We see many ruins from the avenue, but we can't deviate, there's no access from where we are. There are pieces of ruined marble strewn around the ground. There's a column, Trajan's column, with little scenes carved all along the height of it.

At this point I give up on Piazza Navona and the Pantheon, I don't think we can make it there. We head for the Trevi Fountain next. Along the way, we walk through small crowded streets looking for something to eat that's not in the sun and not standing up. And not unbelievably crowded hopefully, which every place seems to be.

Suddenly we see the golden arches. George lights up.

I assent, "Okay, we can go to McDonald's."

It's pretty crowded also but we do it.

They hand me a Coke glass made of glass. I tell them I don't need it. The lady says, "It's a free gift."

I tell her, "We're traveling, it will break, but thank you." That's all I need, to schlep a Coke glass made of glass through Rome the rest of the day. How many of the other people there that day need to carry a glass in their bags?

They charge us for ketchup and mustard.

After lunch we head to the Trevi Fountain, now very close. I had always imagined it as a very large fountain in a very large piazza. Instead it's a very large fountain in a very small piazza. It takes up the entire piazza—there's barely a bit of space to walk around it. It is pretty fabulous. George loves it. He wants to throw a Euro coin in the fountain and we both do.

There are many, many people all around the fountain and a *vigile urbano* who keeps them in check with a whistle. When he whistles everyone looks: you got whistled.

Next we go to the Spanish Steps, really Piazza di Spagna and the Trinita' dei Monti. We get ice cream and I have a confusing experience because I order the Nutella flavor and what I get looks and tastes like *stracciatella*. I'm aggravated but the man selling ice cream to all kinds of people from all over the world has an aggravating job and I don't have the heart to enter into a dispute with him. I try to pawn it on George who likes *stracciatella* and he does trade me for his chocolate ice cream. After a while he decides he made a bad trade and asks to trade back. He gives me my mystery flavor back and by now he's got the melting ice cream dripping all over the cone, so our hands are all sticky.

There is a small fountain at the base of the steps with a little spigot at which people are lined up. We line up too so we can wash the ice cream sticky off our hands.

The Spanish Steps also look different than I expected: I always thought they were more festive but they're not that festive, maybe because it's hot and no one is sitting on the steps in the sun. There are a few people sitting in a sliver of shade and we join them for a while.

Then we climb the steps. Hot. There are vendors selling Louis Vuitton bags along the way.

At the top, there's an obelisk in front of the church, a real Egyptian obelisk. From the top, there's a view of St. Peter's dome in the very distance, so we can say we saw St. Peter's. If it comes up.

We start to make our way back to Roma Termini, the train station. It's a little early for that, but we have done our itinerary and we are exhausted. On the way, we stop by the Piazza del Quirinale. There is a phenomenally attired guard at the door, with long plumes streaming down from his helmet.

~.~.~

On the final leg back to the station we stop to eat something at what looks like a quaint Victorian "tea room." It's near the train station so I should have known that it would be neither Victorian nor a tea room.

A solicitous waiter seats us down. We are seated next to the kitchen door, and someone inside is screaming. I don't really know what he's saying, but our waiter is asking him to keep it down. Asking him repeatedly, and the guy keeps hollering. Our waiter is visibly upset about it.

At a table near the door there is a tall thin man in skinny jeans looking at a laptop. He is wearing a wedding ring and he is sitting with a woman who looks like a hooker. She could be his wife but I don't think so. After a while I realize he owns the place, though when he asks a question no one answers him.

I eat the worst ham sandwich I've ever eaten, and the waiter continues to be very nice—the only sane person in the place.

TOSCANA

We drive south from Florence through the Tuscan countryside. This is the Tuscan scenery that you see in pictures, the little farmhouses at the top of the hill, with the cypresses and the olive trees, with their grayish green color, and the grape vines arranged in rows.

I stop to take some pictures, there are very few people on the road. Tuscany, many people may not know, is a lot like South Dakota. Both are strung with power lines. One side of the road has power lines and the other side has the sun shining at us, so I have fewer opportunities for pictures than I had hoped. I always see these pictures of the Tuscan countryside and I really wanted to take some, so I'm a little disappointed, but still it's a pretty drive. George is a little aggravated because he doesn't understand where we're headed. We're headed to visit my uncle Nardo in Livorno, and I explain that, but as usual he has no sense of time or distance and he doesn't understand why it's taking so long. When he was little he would ask, "What's taking?" Meaning, what's taking so long? In his impatience he abbreviated even the question.

We stop in Montespertoli, a small hilltop village. We find a legal parking space, walk a bit and enter a crowded little bar. I get a cappuccino and George orders a Coca-Cola, which the Tuscans pronounce with aspirated Cs. Who lives in this village? What do these people do? It's very neat and tidy.

We keep going and as we go farther south and west, towards Volterra, the landscape become drier and less pretty. The town of Volterra overlooks this landscape from atop a steep hill. It was a Neolithic settlement, then an Etruscan one. The area is rich in minerals. The town itself is lovely, with stone buildings with many, many little arched windows and the cathedral. For such a small town to have a cathedral is quite special. A brochure from the church indicates that Volterra was the birthplace of San Lino, the first pope after the apostle Peter, so the Catholic tradition goes back nearly 2,000 years. The church itself was first mentioned in writing in 992, over 1,000 years ago, and it was already in existence then, so it's even older, possibly a few centuries older. The brochure contains a lengthy description of the church, both in terms of generic symbolism, what the altar represents, as well as in detail, all the artwork it contains, each of the chapels. The brochure itself is a work of devotion.

Interestingly, the brochure acknowledges both the believer and the tourist as its audience, and it speaks to both. It invites the believer to kneel and pray and the tourist to stop and reflect.

We have once again parked illegally, so we can't linger. As we get back to the car, there is a policeman giving out parking tickets, but he hasn't gotten to us yet, and we take off. We drive down the hill and into a desolate landscape, there's nothing here, just brown hills, it's almost otherworldly. The hilltop town of Volterra separates the pretty countryside from the barren one, it's like something out of Dante.

LIVORNO

We have an appointment to visit my uncle Nardo and my aunt Ilaria in Livorno. Last time I saw them we all went out to lunch, we walked around, we had a fun time. Since then my uncle has had health problems, so I know that we will have a short visit, and that he has a structured life. I am to show up at 2:00 in the afternoon, which places some stress on me since I'm not sure how long it will take me to get there. Nonetheless, good timing or luck gets me there right on time. Ilaria is at the balcony watching for us. They have moved to a bit smaller apartment in a very nice location near the beach.

We go up, and although I knew my uncle was not well, I am not prepared to see him doing as badly as he is doing. He's in a wheelchair and he is very, very thin. Since he's very, very tall, with very long limbs, the effect is shocking. I am happy to see them both, and I try to be upbeat, but I'm devastated.

My aunt has of course gotten some *salatini* and *pasticcini*, some snacks. In my concern to arrive at the time proscribed, I have forgotten to get us lunch, so we are kind of hungry. As I make conversation, George stands behind me at the window and he eats, and it turns out he eats all the *pizzette*, every last one. Oh, my goodness. My uncle's condition, they tell me it's Parkinson's, hasn't affected his appetite, he is enjoying the snacks, though his movements are awkward and stilted. His mind is lucid, but he gets tired. There's not much that he can do. He goes out, pushed in the wheelchair, he watches TV.

He has difficulty talking, he's hard to understand. To tell me how frustrated he is, he thumps his fist on the table and says, "*Vorrei spaccare il mondo*," I want to break the world. This nicest, most intelligent, well educated, well-traveled, wonderful man is trapped in his broken body. It's horrible.

I can barely talk, I tell them about our trip to Florence and Rome. I really want to cry and I do tear up occasionally though I try to hold back the tears. We all pretend I'm not crying, but we all know I am. This is one of the most painful hours of my life, and I only have to live it for an hour.

As we prepare to leave, George picks up the silver Mexican sombrero ashtray. "I remember this." He remembers it from a prior trip. My aunt says, "That's from different times, *altri tempi*." I kiss them goodbye, and when I get back in my car, I cry and cry.

George tells me, "Please don't cry, *mamma*." But I'm just so sad. I will cry for days afterwards too. I just can't stop thinking of him, that look, the table thump.

~.~.~

I will call my uncle Nardo before I leave, and he is pleased, he says kindly, "*Molto gentile*." I have a feeling I will not see him again.

LUNCH WITH PAOLO

My mother's cousin Paolo, comes to my aunt's house for lunch every Wednesday. He is a widower. He comes around a little before lunch time and stays until late afternoon. He has selected the day of the week carefully to avoid his other regularly scheduled commitments, such as the weekly lunch in Ellera with his friend, and to avoid traffic on the Via Aurelia.

This week I mess him up completely because I'm away on Wednesday, but he would like to see us, and so the lunch is moved to Friday. I know he really wants to see us because Friday is bad traffic on the Aurelia. I feel loved.

I brought him a present from America, from my mother, a light green fleece zipper jacket. He opens the package and expresses immediately a concern that the sweater may be too big. He is a tall and very thin man, and he says that everything is always too big, that his aunt gave him a coat in an extra large size that makes him look like a *palombaro*—like a deep sea diver. My aunt confirms that in that coat, when he turns suddenly, he knocks things off tables. I tell him to try on the fleece, and he does, and he is pleasantly surprised that, while roomy, it's not too big.

The present comes with a letter from my mother where she recommends wearing the jacket not as outerwear but as a sweater—under a coat. I imagine it would fit amply under his deep sea diver coat. She also talks in her letter about all the wildlife she sees in her

American yard, because she knows he likes wildlife. He says, "I like wildlife."

"Yes, we know."

To our Italian family our American life is peculiarly odd and intriguingly exotic.

We eat outside. Paolo is notorious for being an exceedingly picky eater, so even with impeccably selected and prepared foods, as you would expect at my aunt's house, he will still not like everything. I remember from another trip that he loves stuffed zucchini, but not the stuffed onions and eggplant that are usually prepared alongside. That's what we have today and he picks carefully to take only the zucchini. Normally this choosy behavior would offend the hostess and be disapproved of, but with him it's understood and accepted. Paolo is a picky eater.

We tell Paolo he has been invited to join us to visit Olivia at her summer home in Naso di Gatto tomorrow. This is way last minute for him, way out of his comfort zone, not how things happen in his life. He immediately says, "I can't. Tomorrow morning I have to go to Albisola."

I quip, "It's not in the morning, it's in the afternoon. You will have to find another excuse."

My aunt laughs and ribs him a little bit.

He ponders, he is feeling cornered at first, then he relaxes and concedes, "I will come along." He considers further, "It will be nice." Deal.

MONTE BEIGUA

The Beigua looms over the seaside. At 1,300 meters, it's 4,000 feet above sea level but it's right there, you can almost touch it.

It's not a peak, it's the high point of a longer mountaintop, but it's easily identifiable by the TV antennas on the summit—when it's not shrouded in clouds.

This morning we have planned to go up there. It's a beautiful sunny day, dazzling... and yet the TV antennas are shrouded in clouds. My aunt is worried, she would prefer we didn't go, but I tell her gently I'm sure the clouds will lift, and if it turns out they don't we'll turn back. She accepts this graciously though I don't believe she believes it. Nor do I believe it myself.

To get to the Beigua we have to drive through the Alpicella, halfway up the mountain, with a view down to the sea and woods all around. We stop at the Alpicella to give the clouds a chance to dissipate, though we can see the clouds still lingering from there. The Alpicella consists of a few houses clustered along the main road, a small parking area with a war memorial, a church, a bar, an elementary school, and a stray dog. There is also a museum, the Esposizione Archeologica Permanente, that we don't visit.

I point out to George that if we lived here he would have gone to school in this school building. He looks at it but has no comment. It may be too far-fetched for him to envision. I wonder what it would be like to live here your whole life. I can't imagine. Do any of the young people still live here their whole life? I've been fortunate to see so much of the world, and I often wonder if the opposite would have been better, to stay in one place always. Not the Alpicella necessarily, but why not? How did I end up in New Jersey and someone else spent his whole life in the Alpicella? I can't explain that.

The little bar is very crowded with men busy chattering. Like all other Italian bars, this is not a dark room but rather an airy place that spills out onto the street. I would like a cappucciono but I'm intimidated by the crowd, I feel too blatantly like someone who has not lived here her whole life, so I pass on the cappuccino for now. It will have to wait.

The clouds still linger over the Beigua but we resume our journey. My aunt had said, "After the Alpicella, turn left." This was counter intuitive because from the Alpicella the Beigua is to the right, but the road has to wind along the mountain to gain the altitude not all at once, so off to the left we go. This stretch of road is very narrow and very twisty and it feels really long. I make with the horn at every turn, one hand on the wheel, one hand on the horn. George is a little embarrassed by my noise making. He wishes we would climb quietly but I can't. It's a scary road. Lovely but scary.

The woods change from conifers, to chestnuts, to beech, patches of one type succeeded by patches of another type. Interestingly, while I expect and fear to suddenly find myself immersed in clouds, there are no clouds here.

There are cars parked along the sides of the road, wherever there's a little flat space. They look perilously close often to falling off the edge. I would not dare to try to park in these spots, but I suspect those that do know what they're doing, they've probably parked in the same spot for years, possibly even for generations. They know exactly where they need to place the wheels.

They probably tell each other, "I park under the chestnut tree, the one by the rock."

"The one by the round rock or the chipped rock?"

"The round rock."

"That's a good position."

These are the cars of the mushroom pickers, it's mushroom picking season in the late, late summer going into September.

We reach the top. We know we're at the top because the road is flat, the scenery is more open, less wooded, and the TV antennas are there, gigantic up close. They have a certain beauty, unexpectedly. They're sculptural, like a modern David, proclaiming the grandeur of our culture.

The air and ambiance at the top are alpine. This is Liguria, the Riviera, but it snows up here in the winter. My aunt will tell my mother on the phone, "*C'e' la neve sul Beigua*," to announce that winter has arrived. There's snow on the Beigua.

And funny enough, now the clouds are below us. We can't see the sea. We skirted the clouds on the way up but they are still there.

There is a lone large building that looks like an alpine refuge, with a restaurant. A little farther there's a little alpine church. We walk towards the restaurant for my delayed cappuccino. As we approach we are barked at vigorously by a little dog unleashed. George is wary of dogs, he's a little afraid, and I try to keep myself between him and the little barking creature. There's no owner around to restrain the dog, to coax him back, to quiet him, he is alone atop the big mountain with the big TV towers, defending from attack of *mamma e bambino*.

We get inside the restaurant and I'm a bit intimidated by the fact that we are the only people there, and it's now late morning and past milk frothing time. Not enough though to renounce cappuccino again. The owner is courteous but not friendly, as you would expect from an alpine man. George gets a can of Coke and a packaged brioche.

We leave the restaurant and walk around. We encounter two hikers, two men in hiking attire, not flashy but hardcore. George is still holding his soda can and one of them says, in Italian, "I'm so thirsty, can I have a sip?"

George looks at him. I can't tell if he is processing, trying to understand, or if he understood and does not want to part with his soda.

I laugh and ask the two men where they hiked from. They came up from the Giovo, it's the pass coming up from the coast to go to Sassello. They plan to hike down to Sassello next. The Giovo to the Beigua on foot, all uphill, is a long hike. Then to Sassello, at least it's downhill, but it's also long.

"When did you leave?" I ask.

"Around 7:30."

It's now late morning. They're a little apologetic, that it took them so long, that they took it easy.

I say something gracious, required by form, but sincerely.

We talk a bit more. They ask where I'm coming from. George hasn't said a word so I don't have to explain that I'm from America but rather I tell them I've come up from the coast.

"*In macchina*," by car, I hasten to explain, and I'm thinking they know that.

I ask about the road ahead and they tell me it's a good road, that it was improved for a bicycle race. Good to know. We part company wishing each other well.

George and I stroll off and, as we had already noticed, we have to watch where we step because the entire top of the Beigua is dotted with sheep poop. By the by, we see the sheep. And suddenly they are coming right at us. I suspect and fear that sheep stampedes are grossly underreported in the media, that they occur tens of times a year, but because they happen in places like up here no one writes about them. I urge someone to take that up, to take up the story of the worldwide problem of sheep stampedes.

I urge George to move off perpendicularly from the moving sheep, and we are safe. There is a grown man shepherd and he looks at us. I'm sure he thinks we're idiots.

~.~.~

There's a trail that runs through the top of the Beigua, and it's a new trail. I show off my knowledge of this trail regularly because all the people who live here have never heard of it. I found out about it from a brochure I picked up in Sassello. As a note, there were no brochures when I was growing up, so brochures are new.

This trail is called the Alta Via dei Monti Liguri, the High Line of the Ligurian Mountains. According to the map in the brochure, it covers the entire long distance of Liguria. Rather than a new trail, it's a rebranding of old trails—I believe most of the trail existed as separate trails that are now one, with a new exciting name and a brochure. I think that this would be a very cool hike to do, the entire thing, but out of our league at least at the moment.

In the meantime, I would like to do a little stretch of it, but I'm confused, because up here the trail is the road itself. There is no trail even though the map says the trail runs through here. What I will find out later is that this stretch of road that coincides with the trail did not exist, there was no road here at one point, there was a trail, and then they paved the trail and it became a road. Both my aunt and my father will tell me that you can't drive from the Beigua to Pra' Rotondo. Well, yes, now you can. You can't hike it.

We don't think about this because now we've known roads all our lives, but this is how roads started, as a trail, then a bigger trail, then maybe a wider path for carts, and so on.

We drive from the Beigua to Pra' Rotondo, and we find that the road is really bad. The hiker said it was good, but it's bad. Everything is really a matter of opinion.

I'm determined to do a little hiking, so we stop along the road a little father along where some other folks are stopped and prepping to go mushroom picking, and start to walk down a trail that leaves off the road, perpendicular to it. A man calls to us, and I turn around. He's all decked out in mushroom picking gear: long pants, boots, walking stick. George and I are wearing shorts and low shoes.

He tells me, "*Signora*, are you walking like that?"

It's a combination of genuine concern, I believe he means well, with a certain amount of judging—he feels the need to tell me that I am not attired and equipped correctly to venture into the woods. He wants me to know I'm doing things wrong.

I assure him we're not going far, just a little ways in. I'm determined to hike. Today. Here. Now. I ask him, "Are there vipers?" That was always the fear when hiking in Sassello: vipers. Vipers and wild boars. He doesn't really confirm that vipers are the danger, he doesn't really explain what the danger is, I'm not sure what it is. Maybe the danger is just people not doing things properly.

Then perhaps he thinks he has offended me, because he assures me that he means well, that he's just trying to help.

I tell him I understand and I appreciate his concern, and we're not going far, we'll be okay, thank you.

And we set down this trail, this is a beautiful little wooded area, very unthreatening, there's no undergrowth, so we can see a distance, we don't feel hemmed in.

Finally, I'm getting my hike. The phone rings. That too would not have happened in the old days. It's the only person who ever calls me, my aunt. Checking in, making sure we're good. I tell her we're running a little behind, we'll probably be late for lunch, please start without me. That's stressful for me, I don't like to be late generally, and I certainly don't like to be late for lunch at someone's house. Then I tell her, truthfully though I'm also trying to get off the phone, that she's coming in and out, I can't hear her all that well, so we hang up.

We keep going, we run into some other hikers, this is hardly a remote place as remote places go. It's beautiful, and George too seems to be enjoying it. Eventually, not that far in, we turn around and get back in the car.

I have plans to drive all the way around, get to Sassello from the other side, and then go home from there. As I'm driving, the phone rings again. It's the only person who ever calls me, my aunt. She says that if I'm in a place with bad reception, as I was on the last call, I need to turn back and get out of there, she's concerned for me. I tell her, we've done that already, we're driving. She's relieved, she's a big worrier.

And from then on, we drive, we drive all the way around, we get to Sassello from the other side, and then go home from there, and we're late for lunch, but it was a good excursion.

THE GATE

My aunt has given me a key to open the main gate, so I can go in and out with the car. The key works going out, but I can't get it to work coming back in. It just will not open the gate for me. There are no other keys, apparently, and she doesn't really believe that the key doesn't work. And surely it would not be the first time I had key problems, I don't do well with keys. In any case, I have to buzz her on the intercom, the *citofono*, every time I come back.

I buzz, and from inside, through the intercom, she always asks, "*Chi e?*" Who is it?

"*Sono Olga.*" It's Olga.

"*Chi e'? Non sento niente.*" She can't hear anything.

Louder, "*Sono Olga.*"

"*Non sento.*" This happens every time.

Very loud, "*Sono Olga!*"

At this point George in the back seat of the car is screaming too, "*Sono Olga, sono Olga, sono Olga.*" He thinks it's hilarious.

But she still can't hear, and then I hear her saying to herself, "I don't hear anything. I'll open the gate anyway." And she buzzes me in.

NASO DI GATTO

We have been invited to Naso di Gatto by my mother's friend Olivia who has recently set up a small summer home there. She tells us all about it all the time, that it's such a wonderful place, she's very excited to show it to us and we're interested in seeing it. The little excursion has turned into an extravaganza that includes my aunt and Paolo, and now Ginevra is going as well. The average age of the party excluding me and George is in the mid-70s.

We have to pick Ginevra and Paolo up along the way. I speak to Ginevra on the phone and I tell her we'll stop by her house. She says, "No, no, I will wait for you on the Aurelia, where the Conad supermarket used to be." Funny enough, I actually know where that is. I assure her I don't mind driving the extra 200 meters up the hill to pick her up at her door but she will not be budged. I don't get this at all, but fine. Sure enough, she is there waiting for us and gets in the car.

Then we have to pick up Paolo, and my aunt had suggested we pick him up at the Torretta—nowhere near his apartment building. I proposed that we pick him up at his apartment building instead, and she agreed that mine was a better plan. I speak to him on the phone and I tell him we'll ring the intercom when we get there, and he can come downstairs. He says, "No, no, I will wait for you downstairs in the street." You know what? Fine. I don't get it, but sure enough, he is there waiting for us and gets in the car.

I tell him he will have to direct me now, I'm counting on him to get us there because we believe as a group that he is the one who knows where it is. And he does. If we did need directions, they would be, "Drive to the Santuario, and then keep going straight." Thank goodness we don't need them.

We drive inland, which means we drive uphill. Way uphill, with many hairpin turns. Naso di Gatto is at 700 meters—2,000 feet—and that's what makes it pleasantly cool in the summer. It's a pass, the high point on the road, it's surrounded by woods. We get there, after all the climbing and all the hairpin turns and all the anticipation. And what it consists of is the road itself, wide at this spot, plus along the road I count three buildings and a chicken coop. That's it.

We park randomly on the side of the road, the only place in Liguria with all the parking you wish for. Olivia runs out to greet us, she appears immediately out of nowhere. She is so excited to see us. We walk with her to the side of one of the buildings, under a *pergola*, a grape arbor, a wide one. The structure of the arbor is metal, with a pole in the middle, about 20 feet wide, quite large, and shady from the vines. Underneath the arbor are tables and chairs.

Past the arbor is Olivia's place—a small and meticulously planned apartment on the ground floor, accessible directly from the outside. Paolo remarks on the solid door with multiple bolts, and George loves the anti-fly curtain consisting of strings of pompons. He will play with this throughout the visit, the highlight of the trip for him, though for him too, this place is soothing and pleasant—there's nothing to do, but he doesn't complain.

Olivia is famously friends with an architect, and he helped her fix up the apartment and decorate it. The main room has a long wooden table, a brand new but old-fashioned stove and a light gray marble sink like my grandmother had in her apartment. It's very nice and I can see why she loves it here, with the cozy apartment and the grape arbor outdoors.

Olivia explained to us that this is an old place, associated with her family. She has relatives in the same building, next door to her. In the old days this was a dormitory for hunters who used to come up from Savona. It's a completely unknown little gem, even the locals don't know about it—there's nothing here but it's special, and it is cooler. Only Paolo among us had been here before, he used to come up on Sunday drives with his wife and their dog.

After the tour of the indoors we return outside, where Olivia has prepared some specialties. She has pieces of focaccia topped with chunks of lard. I love focaccia but the lard I could do without, but I eat it—I eat the lard in one gulp. She also made apple slices caked in dough and fried. These are delicious and they have their own lore, as all food tends to do. They should be made with *mele renette*, these may not be *renette*, but Paolo's scarfing them, so evidently they will do. She also serves a salad and fruit salad and wine and dessert. We sit under the grape arbor, eating fried apples, it's lovely.

The tables and chairs under the arbor are communal, for the whole building. Some of the other residents are sitting a few feet away and occasionally we make small talk with them, but only at that distance and infrequently. Just enough to stay on good terms, not enough to get friendly. And we don't invite them to join in the feast. That's the protocol clearly, they're not sitting there saying they can't believe we're not inviting them to join us. They could be saving it for later but I don't think so.

Later Olivia's relatives come by and she introduces us. Clearly they enjoy each other's company up here. This is what they do, they hang out, the weather is cool, and they chat and play cards. What else can one want?

~.~.~

I drop off Ginevra and Paolo in Savona, expecting to see them both again next year. I will see Ginevra, but I have no idea now that I will never see Paolo again.

PIANI D'INVREA

We go to the beach at the Piani d'Invrea. This is a rocky section of the coast where the train used to run right along the water. The train line has been moved, and now there is a walkway called the Lungomare Europa, with tiny rocky coves with free access to the water. Most people do not come here to go to the beach, so it's kind of cool.

Over the years we have stopped at various different coves, we have some favorites. The rocks are great for climbing, the water is clear, it's lovely.

I've met different people along here. I met a woman who used to come here when she was a child, in *colonia*. A *colonia estiva* was a summer camp for poor children who were sent to the beach from the interior to live in huge very serious looking buildings and go to the beach during the day. She was here with her daughter, visiting her brother who lived here at the shore, and she tried to talk to George but I had to explain to her that we lived in America and that he doesn't speak Italian. She struck up the conversation, which was unusual. I wasn't all that interested in getting to know her, but she was nice, it was okay.

I met a young American woman once, very pregnant, who lived here with her husband. She enjoyed speaking English with me, but she seemed to enjoy Italy. She struck up the conversation, which I would expect—an American would want to talk.

Today we stop at a particular small cove. There are a few other people. Near us, there is a couple, a man and a woman, middle aged, very sedate. On the other side of them is a mother and daughter, the mother is elderly and thin and wearing a black one piece bathing suit and a hat, and the daughter is middle aged and not too thin and wearing a black bikini.

The couple nearest us pull out a lunch and eat sandwiches right there on the beach. After lunch, the woman, who is rotund, enters the water and swims out about 10 feet.

The elderly woman on the other side of the couple turns to the woman's husband and says to him, "She just ate." In other words, she can't go swimming now, she just ate and she will have a seizure and drown. It's that judging quality again on display, they would not necessarily strike up a conversation, but the woman has to tell the man they're doing things wrong. And the swimmer is very close to the beach and she floats quite well, there's really no danger here. But she needs to be told, she's behaving wrong.

GIOVO

I'd like to take another shot at the Alta Via dei Monti Liguri. The trail runs through the Giovo, which is the pass on the way to Sassello, the pass between the coast and the interior where Sassello is. We drive up to the Giovo in the afternoon, park, and find the Alta Via. We start along the trail. It's through woods, pretty woods, with not much undergrowth. I could go off the trail and start to look for mushrooms, but I don't.

The trail is very well marked. The old markers are there too, simple one-color markers. The Alta Via marker is in three colors. When you think about that, someone went along all these trails with three different paint colors to mark the trail. Did they have to wait for each one to dry? There are many, many markings, not just where someone might be confused as to which way to go, but all along the trail. The marker looks like a Canadian flag, but instead of the red maple leaf there are the letters AV in black in the center. We go up quite a ways, there's not much of a view, because there are trees on both sides.

George doesn't see the point really, he's on a complaining kick, he wants to go back. Eventually we turn back. We'll come back here someday and go all the way up to the Beigua on this trail. Ha! We will. I sometimes feel like our entire trip is fixing to get ready for another trip.

MONTECARLO AND MENTONE

"George, we're going to France today."

"I don't want to go to France."

"We're going to France and to Montecarlo, which is a different country, so we'll be in three countries in a single day."

"I don't want to go to France or Montecarlo."

"Okay, let's go."

We stop at an *autogrill* and he gets cookies, packaged in a long thin cylinder. As I drink my cappuccino I look to my left and I see a biker couple looking behind me with a horrified look. Oh-oh, what did George do? What he did is struggle to open the package so the package exploded and some of the cookies fell on the floor. The source of the horror is that he is picking them up off the floor and putting them back in the package.

I try to pretend that I'm pro hygiene and I ask him which ones fell on the floor.

"The broken ones."

"Okay, then, let's throw those out, shall we?" I make a big show of throwing them out so the biker observers will see.

He has salvaged the majority, I don't know if truly because they did not fall on the floor, or because he saw me throwing them out and pretended they were clean.

The young woman behind the counter came out to sweep the crumbs and she was really very nice about the whole thing, the incident didn't seem to phase her at all. George was quite mortified, not so much by the accident, which he was easily addressing by putting all the cookies back in the package, but by all the attention.

We get to France. Along the way I am honked at furiously by a woman in a small old car who firmly believes that I ran a yield sign. It is not my impression that I did that, but it's possible I suppose. She is gesticulating wildly in her little car, trying to convey to me what a horrible driver I am. George will later refer to this single incident as, "You were constantly getting honked at all the time."

We get to Monaco, our third country of the day.

My cousin had told me a few things to know about Montecarlo, such as: there is lots of parking. This is true. Not that I doubted it, but it's true. There are express roads that cut through the city, and there are parking garages indicated throughout, with illuminated numbers enumerating, I think, the available parking spaces. There are many available parking spaces in many garages. There are so many in fact that I don't know what to do. I am not psychologically prepared for parking largesse, surely I don't deserve it and so much parking good fortune can't be happening to me.

I see some signs directing traffic to the palace and museums, and I decide to follow those, expecting all along to end up on a dead-end street in a pedestrian zone inches from a cliff in the next town. Instead I end up at the bottom of the old town, in the Parking du Chemin des Pecheurs, a romantic name for a garage. Never have I been this fortunate with parking.

Although, as it happens, I had been to this parking garage before. Yes, I had. My aunt and uncle some 20 years ago, when I was young, took me to Montecarlo for the day and ended up parked right here. They had hated the underground parking and vowed never to return, but here I am, so happy to be so well situated. I park in a row reseved for electric cars, but none of the other vehicles appear to be electric either. In fact, one says Diesel on the side, so I go for it.

We emerge from the garage right in front of the Aquarium! Pardon me, the Aquarium and Oceanographic Institute. George loves aquariums. The day is looking good, this will be one of those moments of joy for him. The museum is open every day except the day of the Formula 1 race, which is not today.

At the ticket window I speak French, *"Deux. Pour moi et l'enfant."* I am so cool.

The ticket vendor proceeds to say something I don't understand, and he gives me the tickets.

The aquarium is very cool and the oceanographic institute part of the building is chock full of items. What's super cool is the building itself, an ornate building perched on a cliff overlooking the Mediterranean. There's a rooftop restaurant that we don't patronize.

On the same cliff overlooking the sea, along with the aquarium, there is the old town and the palace. This is different from the rest of Montecarlo that has many newer and taller buildings.

We exit and make our way into the old town. The old town is all pale pink and it has little tiny streets. The street names are in French and Genoese. The tiny streets are lined with stores and food places.

We stop in a sandwich shop and I point to my selection of food. I point in French, *"Ceci."*

The vendor says something I of course don't understand. I point more earnestly to the one I want. The sandwich is delicious: *prosciutto crudo* in a focaccia bread.

We walk out to the palace square and I tell George this is where the prince lives. He's flabbergasted, "Princes still exist?"

"Yes, they do. There are not many, but yes."

I'm looking at him and I can see his brain is working. He's reviewing everything he knows about life and reality and trying to reorganize it based on this new information. He's wondering, What else am I completely wrong about? Why don't people tell me things?

This exchange piggy backs on an ongoing discussion we have about dragons, and whether they ever existed. I tell him no, but he keeps approaching it from different angles to see if he can determine the whole truth.

"Dinosaurs don't exist today but they did in the past."

"Yes, but we have dinosaur bones, which you've seen. No one has ever found an old dragon bone."

This new information about princes may really reopen the whole dragon thing. Not only might dragons have existed after all, but how do we know they're not still around today?

My cousin had suggested we see the changing of the guard at the palace. We are standing in front of the palace, looking at the guard, and suddenly two guards emerge from the palace, one of the bellowing orders to the other. It's 1:00 in the afternoon and they are changing the guard! We see the changing of the guard. I ask George if he wants to take a tour of the palace but he declines.

We walk along the side of the cliff through the Jardin Exotique, a lovely Mediterranean garden with walkways and flower beds and benches and a fountain. It's so beautiful that it's hard to soak up as much as you feel you should.

On the way back to Italy from Montecarlo we stop in Menton, the only town between Montecarlo and Italy. The French spell it Menton and pronounce it Mahntone, the Italians spell it Mentone and pronounce it Mayntonay. The Genoese likely have a third pronunciation for it, maybe Mayntoon.

My cousin had said to go to the old port, and we do.

We stop for ice cream and I want to speak French but I don't know how to say "*coppetta*" in French. It turns out the vendor speaks both French and Italian. I ask her how to say "*coppetta*" and she says, "*Pot*." Pronounced "poe," as in Edgar Allan. So now I know.

SASSELLO

At the end of August for the feast of San Giovanni the fair comes to Sassello. This consists of a market that fills every nook and cranny of the town, including the bocce court.

This was always a highlight of the summer, the fair, and this year we happen to chance on it. We go to Sassello, and the market is here. On the one hand, all these stands are intrusive. On the other hand, it's exciting, this is a big deal, the town is very crowded, people come from all around. There is no place to park, even less place to park than usual, because the bigger parking area in the square is also taken over by the market.

I look at all the wares, and I buy two scarves, one lime green and one hot pink. The woman who sells them to me makes a point of telling me what fibers they're made of—the pink one is wool, the green one is *viscosa*. Even at the street market, she knows she'll be back next year, and I'm sure she doesn't want me to complain then that one wasn't wool.

We stop at another vendor that sells candy—you can fill a bag yourself with any mix from many bins, all different candies, sold by weight. F.A.O. Schwartz in New York has the exact same setup with their selection of candy. It's a real kid catcher—George loves it. He and I spend a long time making our selections, and we start eating as we walk away.

Italians do not sell their used stuff at yard sales. It would be mortifying for both the seller and the buyer, people would talk about them and pity them for being destitute. But a kid is selling a few of his toys today, on the feast day, and he's aggressive about it too, though we keep moving.

Years later George will ask me, "What's Popeye called in Italian?"

"Braccio di Ferro."

"A kid was selling a Braccio di Ferro toy in Sassello."

FAREWELL DINNER

My cousin Nino and his wife Linda are coming to dinner with their very tall son again tonight. Gianni's son is coming too. Nino's son has spent a month in Boston this summer at a program at a university. This was a super cool experience for him—that curiosity and fascination with America—and he likes to talk about it.

At dinner he's sitting across from George and he tells his two top stories: one involves doing laundry and the other cleaning his room. These are clearly two things that he doesn't do at home. He went all the way to Boston to experience the exoticism of running a washer. I find this hilarious.

The other often told tale from his trip is about his swim in the Atlantic Ocean. He came out of the water yelling, "*Viva l'Italia!*" The water was so much colder than the one of the Mediterranean!

After dinner the boys go downstairs to play ping pong. When they come back Nino tells me that George didn't want to play. I knew that, George can't play ping pong, but watching the big boys play—what a treat! George is beaming.

Linda says, "This can become our tradition, the end of summer dinner." I hope so, I hope that life allows us to make it an ongoing event. It's a signal of the differences between us: she feels confident that we will do the same thing again and again, I tend to think events will get in the way.

THE GARDEN AND THE ATTIC

We go out to the garden for a special tour, I want to take pictures of my aunt's garden to take back to my mother. My aunt's garden is like a Mediterranean park, with palm trees, many varieties of palm trees, and small walks and steps. She continues to plant, change and add, she's very into her garden. She just added rosemary bushes, lots of them, that cascade down. It's a spectacular garden. I take pictures of her in it to take back to my mother.

Other people's gardens are always a pleasure, my own garden makes me crazy.

Then we go upstairs to the top level of the house, and we poke around through all the things up there. My grandfather's naval uniforms are there, George tries on the hats. He won't put on the epaulets, which are very heavy and made of metal. I always thought epaulets were made of soft fabric, but these are metal. They're very cool. I take pictures of him wearing my grandfather's hats.

There's also a little toy furniture set that I recognize, it was in my grandmother's house. It's a little table and chairs with a flower motif. It belonged to my mother and my aunt when they were children. There are also, mysteriously, postcards sent from my high school boyfriend to his parents from various trips he took. I ask her if I can have them and she says sure. They're not really hers and they're not really mine either. I don't know why they're here at all. It's like a jumble of memories, like someone threw up a bunch of memories in the air and they fell haphazardly, here are mine, here are yours, here are someone else's.

And yet my memories, all mixed up with the present, are what I am. Aleksandar Hemon talks about how his native Sarajevo and his current hometown of Chicago blend together, and how returning to Chicago from Sarajevo is returning home, from home. That speaks to me, that's how I feel.

And we go home again, we return home from home.

THE CHICKENS OF FRENCHTOWN

Frenchtown is a sleepy little town in New Jersey, down the road from my house. It has an old train line that's now a walking and biking trail along the Delaware River.

Along the trail there's a house with a chicken coop with a dozen chickens of different varieties: speckled black and white ones, little brown ones, fluffy white ones, classic caramel colored ones, and a big rooster.

Italian roosters say, "Chicchirichi'," pronounced keekeereekee, and hens say, "Coccode'," cocoaduh. I think the Frenchtown chickens speak Italian.

A chicken's life seems pleasant, but at times you see that they too have their burdens. At one point, a new bunch of little white chickens is added to the coop. These little new arrivals stick to each other like glue, they go everywhere together, and the other chickens harass them, chase them and peck at them.

Sometimes the chickens, in one body, walk up to us. They probably just think we are going to feed them, but a hungry chicken looks a lot like an angry chicken, it's hard to discern chicken facial expressions, and we amscray.

I always drag George out of the house for an after dinner stroll with the excuse of going to see the chickens. The excitement of the chickens wears out after the first two or three times, but I keep taking him for our evening stroll. It becomes a tradition, our little tradition. I tell him, "Someday you will remember these walks, and tell your grandchildren about them, 'I used to go for a walk in the evening with my mother—along the Delaware river, to see the chickens. The evenings were beautiful, the light was golden.'"

The wild honeysuckle on the edge of the walking trail smells sweet.

TRIP V: INDEPENDENCE

"Ma, cipressetti miei, lasciatem'ire:
Or non e' piu' quel tempo e quell'eta'."
                      Giosue' Carducci

But, my little cypress, let me go:
It's not that time anymore, or that age.

THEY'RE NOT THERE ANYMORE

In late July my mother's cousin Paolo went into the hospital. He had fallen, and then he got pneumonia. My aunt visited him and brought him things he needed, he was getting better. My mother had talked to him shortly before he got sick, and told him about an article in The New Yorker that she read, about opera, Paolo's great love. She translated the article for him and mailed it to him. She also knit him a scarf for me to bring him when I went again.

Then suddenly my mother received a call that he died.

Paolo, the slightly eccentric widower, the picky eater, skinny as a rail, suddenly died. My mother attributed it to weakness due to lack of food, she thinks he didn't eat enough. I don't know. She's wondering where the letter is, he never read it. And she doesn't know what to do with the scarf.

The suddenness of it, the fact that he's one of her last living relations, saddens her deeply. She brings him up again and again.

In the middle of August, my uncle Nardo, who had been very sick for a couple of years, whom I saw myself last year in a terrible state, also died. This was maybe less sudden, he could not talk to my father on the phone anymore, we knew he was not well, but it was still a big shock and very sad.

He was a wonderful man, so kind and gentle, a wonderful human being. And tall. With his death the average height of the population has diminished. While I didn't know Paolo well, I knew my uncle Nardo well and I adored him.

Two people whom I went to see, who were part of the reason I went to Italy, are gone.

DOLCEACQUA AND PIGNA

There's a town above Ventimiglia, all the way over, almost in France, that's famous for its medieval bridge. Though in fact the original medieval bridge was destroyed. The one that we are looking at right now is the new one, rebuilt in the 15th century. I imagine that the people in the 15th century looked at it, shook their heads and said, "It's just not the same. It looks so new. It's missing that charm of the medieval one." Or most likely they said, "Oh good, I don't have to walk through the river anymore." Since progress was slow, they may have welcomed progress.

Nonetheless, some 400 years later, Claude Monet saw the bridge and liked it very much, he called it a "jewel of lightness." There's a wooden plaque commemorating his visit. I wonder if he knew that it was a replacement bridge. Nonetheless, he did get it right, it is a jewel of lightness, a high thin arch.

He painted two pictures of it, one of them was sold at auction in 2000 for over $700,000, and the other one is in the Clark in Williamstown, MA. We visited the Clark earlier this year and I think that's what brought us here today. Dolceacqua's medieval bridge that's not medieval was made famous for all time by a French painter who was there one day in 1884 whose painting is now located in the most remote part of Massachusetts. Incredible.

Not only is the bridge medieval, or at any rate a 600-year old pseudo medieval reproduction, but the whole town is medieval as well. We walk inside of it, and it's a maze of tiny streets between tall buildings. The buildings are propped apart with arches strung between them at various heights above our heads. Some of the streets are covered overhead, they're actual tunnels. It feels like a magical place, and in fact George thinks it's like Diagon Alley in Harry Potter. I tell him, "It's not every day that you can walk through a magical medieval town." He sort of reluctantly acknowledges that to be the case.

There's an impressive castle above the town, a big castle guarding a narrow little valley of no apparent value. We walk up to the castle, which is open for visitors, and it's closed for lunch. So we go to lunch.

We cross the bridge to the newer part of town and sit at an outdoor restaurant. It's under big white umbrellas so it's a little shaded, but it's very hot. There are two women who are serving the whole place, it's a pretty big restaurant, with many tables occupied. One brings us the menu and we pick quickly what we want. And then we are completely ignored. They bring food out to other people, they chat, they go back and forth, and they ignore us completely. A bit of time goes by. I think to myself, we can leave now. If we order, and then it takes a long time, we can't leave anymore. So we get up and leave. I'm a little embarrassed and George is more embarrassed than I, but we get up and leave. We go to a bar nearby and eat a *pizzetta* and a focaccia. Simple, cheap, quick, on our terms.

I extricate my car from the parking space I put it in, with much difficulty. If I got in, I should be able to get out, but getting out seems to require a whole other set of skills, skills I don't have. I make George stand outside the car and indicate with the distance between his hands what the distance is between me and the other cars. He takes this role very seriously, with his little hands. It makes me laugh and I still can't get out. Finally I do, I try something else, a different twist of the car, and it works. We are out of here. Someone immediately takes my spot.

I don't want to retrace my steps, back down towards the Aurelia, so we head uphill. We get to Pigna. It's not as magical as Dolceacqua, the streets are not quite as narrow and the buildings don't close above your head quite as much. Not as much, but they still do. We get to an area that looks like an old marketplace, an outdoor area covered with an arched ceiling. A cat walks by. Two men are talking.

The church is adjacent. I think it's Saint George, I thought I saw the telltale dragon carved above the doorway, but it's Saint Michael, the archangel. One of those saints keeping the world safe for Christianity. Inside, as usual, it's beautiful, very ornate. Every little town always has a fabulous church.

We leave. We should, we will find out, drive back down, the way we came, towards the coast. But the map shows we can explore, we can do a loop uphill and head back down towards the coast by another road. This is not the first time I am cruelly deceived by a map. I should know better. The road uphill is very, very long, very, very narrow and very, very curvy. It's awful. I honk at every turn. Thankfully there are very few people coming the other way. It's awful but I keep going. Why do I do that? We can see to the right how far up we are. We are going along a fairly high mountain, a wooded mountain.

I tell George everything is fine, we are doing well. He will tell me later that he thought I was a little stressed.

"Why did you think that?"

"You kept saying, 'Oh, my God.'"

And I thought I was so cool.

The road seems endless, it just keeps going and going, up and up, around this mountain. We are on the valley side of the road, the valley is to our right. The people coming down are at least on the mountain side, in a wreck they would scrape the mountain, not fall off as we would do. Near the top, after really a hair-raising drive, a downright dangerous drive, we see a sign: "No protection downhill for 3 kilometers." So now they are telling us officially, this is a very dangerous road. Up until this point, no biggie. Now watch out. Oh, my God.

At the top, we stop. I have to breathe. We are way, way up. We can see a very long distance, down the wooded valley. A motorcycle with a man and a woman stop to ask me for directions. I cannot imagine doing that road on a motorcycle, but they don't seem too stressed, other than they're not sure where they are. I tell them I don't really know where we are either, but I have a map I can share.

I take the map out of the car, I show them roughly where I think we are, and they are satisfied. They take off.

I take off too. The road down in comparison is wonderful, still through woods but considerably wider. And we are on the mountain side of the road, the safer side.

Adventure comes in many ways, sometimes really unexpectedly. I'm not looking for adventure here, but here it is, I feel we were at risk. The Aurelia is a peach in comparison.

GENOVA

We are going to the aquarium in Genova today. It's the second largest in Europe, and it's supposed to be quite nice as well as crowded.

We take the train. The train makes every stop including all the Genova ones: Genova Voltri, Genova Pra, Genova Pegli, Genova Sestri, Genova Cornigliano, Genova Sampierdarena and finally our stop, Genova Principe. A young couple with a tennis racquet asks me how long to their stop. I must look like a local, which I'm not, so I have to tell them I don't know. They look like they don't believe me, a woman with a young child and no baggage, where could I possibly be from?

We get off the train and follow the crowd. Evidently everyone in Genova is headed to the aquarium, a short walk from the station. There's a short line, but not a terrible one. The people in front of us tell us it's usually much worse. It's a Monday, so maybe an off day.

Inside the aquarium, it's crowded, though as we progress it gets less so, it kind of thins out. It's quite an important aquarium, I can see why, there are many, many tanks with many, many fish in each one. There's one section that's set up so it feels like you're on the deck of a ship, looking down into the sea. Everyone is taking pictures of the fish, something I completely don't get. Who needs a picture of a fish? Do you look at it later on? Ah, yes, I remember that fish, it was a memorable fish.

After the aquarium, we go to the Museo del Mare, nearby. This is also an important institution, yet nearly deserted. It's kind of sad, because there's a lot here, well curated, someone has put a lot into the exhibits. The building is an ancient building from the 1600s with a modern addition.

They start with Columbus and at first I think they're milking it. This whole tourist part of Genova was renovated for the occasion of the 500th anniversary of Columbus's voyage to America, in 1992. But there's so much more than Columbus, including actual life size boats and an exhibit about emigration, not a topic normally discussed much in Italy. The experience of the emigrants is displayed room by room of the inside of the ship where they would have sailed.

We spend a lot of time here, it's kind of soothing and stimulating both.

Outside again, we see a bus headed to a destination called Vannucci, my last name. It turns out that there's a street in Genova named after an Atto Vannucci, a writer, teacher, historian unknown to me but with his own entry in the Italian Wikipedia. There is a famous Vannucci, Pietro Vannucci, the renaissance painter better known as Il Perugino, with his own street in his native Perugia, Corso Vannucci.

~.~.~

We walk back to the station down a narrow alley of, semi-appropriately, immigrant shops. Arab and Latin food, money transfers, cheap goods, it's like being in New York. We catch the train back just barely and hit all the Genova stops in reverse order.

A PARTY ON A BOAT

We are invited to a party on a boat, a small party with a few adults and two other children, a girl about George's age, and a younger boy. Like all Italian children, they are learning English, and George, being like he always is, is completely ungracious about it. While he is genuinely a kind and caring person, he can only be kind and caring when it's genuine. He does not understand that he has to pretend to be kind and caring when the feeling isn't there. As Sheldon Cooper could tell him, "It's not optional."

We adults are kind of joking about it, that the kids aren't talking. Then the mother walks over to them, at their kids' table, and comes back to say, "I told her to ask George about sports." It's funny because while Italians don't seem to talk about sports very much, it's certainly a great topic of conversation with American children. Except with George. While all American children, it seems, play a sport, George has no interest in sports and, like me, he's not good at them. He's also not competitive. And it generally aggravates me that parents extoll the athletic virtues of their children while I don't usually share his excellent grades. Not here though, I'm not aggravated at anything that's being said, I just wish George would make an effort.

By the by, he comes by, rubs his cheek against mine, trying to get my attention like a cat might. Then he spills ice cream on his clean shirt. He's an ornery kid and a slob tonight. Under the stars outside, among the twinkling lights of the harbor, the town, the other boats. It's a magical night regardless.

SESTRIERE

We are back in Sestriere, a place George really likes. I think he likes it because it's peaceful and because it's just he and I, so he doesn't have to endure Italian. It's going to be a few days of hikes up the mountains and strolls around town. That's it. Nice.

Our first hike is to the Chisonetto, a small rustic restaurant on the ski slopes that's open to hikers in the summer. We hear bells as we get closer. Sure enough, we come upon and walk through a flock of sheep, a large flock of sheep. They all amble together across the steep mountainside. I don't see a shepherd, but there is a very active sheep dog who manages them terrifically well. He runs around them barking and they move as he wishes them to. It's fantastic to watch, it's like something you would watch on TV on a nature show, with a voice over explaining what the dog is doing. Only there is no explanation and none is needed, it's clear what the dog is doing.

I pose George for a few pictures in front of the sheep because I think it's so cool, when will he again get this close to this many sheep? He does not find it at all worthy, and he's scowling in all the pictures.

After our hike, we head into town for a stroll and some dinner. The afternoon stroll is a tradition, and we amble with all the other amblers, here and there looking at shop windows. We sit on a bench and watch a group of kids playing. They are all about George's age, maybe ten to twelve years old, with one much taller kid. I can't tell if the taller kid is older or just big. They are plotting a scheme to throw water balloons at some friends, soon to be not friends if the plan succeeds, as they come out of the movies. One kid is the leader, referred to by the others as Lo Stratega. Since they need to wait for the movie to let out, the preparations are long and the wait is suspenseful, kind of an Alpine kid High Noon. When they movie does finally let out, there's some scurrying, but I don't see any attack. It turns out that the big kid tipped off the intended targets. The rest of them are mad at him, and he tells them, "Go ahead and attack me instead then," a completely unexpected twist. I did not see that coming, and neither did they. Nor did they have any interest in that, it just wasn't the same. They dispersed.

We had to wait until 7 o'clock for the pizza place to open, a long wait. We had a very nice pizza, mine with cheese and a cured meat, George's plain. A nice day, with tomorrow more of the same.

~.~.~

The plans for the next day are to go to the restaurant at the Alpette. This is a very close-by hill, right in front of the town, it looks easy, but as usual topography fools me. There is a winding road up, but it's long so instead we go straight uphill, up the ski slope, a difficult hike. It's at 2,300 meters, up 300 meters from the town, about 1,000 feet. We get there, I get the polenta *concia*, with various cheeses, and I make George get a lasagna. I make him because I know he will love it and he does, he eats it joyfully.

A couple arrives, complaining to all those within earshot that the hike up was very tough. They turn to me and ask if I drove up. Excuse me? Did I drive up? Do I look like I drove up? Obviously I do. "No," I say, "we walked up the ski slope, the *pista*." In other words, we came up the hardest way. They look away without saying anything, they don't want to know me, someone who looks like she had to have driven up and who actually walked up the *pista*. What does it say about them?

A father and son team arrives, they biked up, not up the *pista* but up the winding road, still a fairly grueling bike ride. They are cheerful about it and chat everyone up.

We leave and I decide to return to town a different way, towards the back of the mountain. In the process, we go a long way back and all the way to the dam, which is dry this time of year, a very long way back.

On our stroll into town we come across the gang of kids again. This time they are playing a game involving colors, and, much as I observe them, I can't figure it out. It's something like: if you have the color named you're it, or if you don't have it, you're it. I wonder if I were to observe a chess game for the first time how long it would take me to figure out the moves. So that's how the knight moves!

It's tough to wait until 7 for dinner, so instead we picnic. I buy some *prosciutto* and some bread in a little tiny food store right on the main square, and we sit outside to eat our dinner. It's kind of nice.

~.~.~

This morning we are going in the opposite direction, up the back of the town, towards the Fraiteve. George is not in the mood, at all. I trick him all the way up by telling him that we're not going far, when in fact we will end up going farther than even I expected to. We are walking up a road that zig zags up the side of the mountain, in large zig zags. We come to a sheep pen, with the sheep penned in, not roaming free like the prior day.

It's interesting to me that in spite of the preponderance of sheep everywhere in Italy, or almost everywhere, or at least on most of the high ground, it's oxen that have inspired wisdom through the ages. A saying in my mother's family that I have only heard in my family suggests that *chi ha perso i buoi non viene a cercarli qua*, those that lost their oxen will not come looking for them here. It means that there's no need to be overly particular. This is hilarious on multiple levels. First of all, who loses their oxen? They're kind of big, and do they run amok? Second, why would they in fact their owners come here to look for them? And finally, why is it that people that tend to lose their oxen are considered especially particular? It would seem that oxen losers, or oxen keepers for that matter, would tend to specifically not be overly particular. If you are overly particular you don't select oxen keeping as a life pursuit.

This is applied to mundane tasks such as dusting or ironing, if the task is performed less than perfectly, *chi ha perso i buoi* won't be looking for them here. It's interesting to me as someone who doesn't iron, and who dusts infrequently, that anyone would care how well those tasks are done, they're not important, why even bother invoking the oxen losers. But even today, women seem to still have self-worth tied up in a clean house.

Another saying involving oxen is the one that recommends *mogli e buoi dei paesi tuoi*, spouses and oxen from your own homeland. This is one that I should well have heeded myself, though it did not ring true to me early on.

And the great poet Carducci wrote a famous poem that begins with *T'amo pio bove*, I love you pious ox. He goes on to say that the ox is solemn and patient.

It may be that oxen were valued in the old days, as wealth and security. Hercules drove cattle across the Alps as one of his labors. And it seems that Hannibal crossed the Alps not so much to surprise the Romans, who knew he was there—it's hard to hide tens of thousands of people and thousands of horses on the march—as much as he wanted to be viewed as the new Hercules, such was the importance of his transalpine cattle drive.

~.~.~

I'm unsure of what's back here, on this part of the mountain, because we've never hiked up this way. I run into three people who have a trail map, what a novel concept. I ask them if there's a restaurant up this way, and they tell me there is a ways away, and at 2,400 meters. They mention this altitude to me with a tone that clearly indicates I could never, ever walk up that high. It's possible that I always convey this wimpy image because I carry a pocketbook rather than a backpack. It could be that, it could be that I'm a mother with a child, I don't know what it is that makes everyone always underestimate me.

We keep going and we never do go to the restaurant, though not because it's too far a climb, but rather because the mountain is deserted. We are traveling horizontally now, and we stop a man on a bicycle to ask him what's ahead. There's another restaurant in our horizontal direction, not too far, he says. I thank him and apologize for making him stop. He's fine with it.

We keep going and encounter a couple as the only other travelers on this trail, which is beautiful. I comment to them how beautiful the trail is, and how deserted, I tell them I find it a little creepy. The woman tells me that yesterday her husband walked on ahead and they lost each other. That would be terrifying, if that happened to me and George, that would be like a horrible nightmare.

Under the trees, little dead branches are arranged in little piles—by whom and for what purpose I cannot imagine.

We get to a tub in the middle of the woods here. This is a drinking fountain for cows I believe, and sure enough a little later on we encounter a man with some dogs and a small herd of cows, maybe a dozen on so. They are not very close to us, or coming in our direction, thankfully, because they are way scarier than sheep, they're bigger and they move pretty fast. The man is hollering at them, that's his cow management technique. I can't tell if it's working: they are moving, but he seems to be dissatisfied as evidenced by the continuation of the hollering. I hear it and the cow bells as they get fainter and fainter, and it never seems to stop.

We get to a small restaurant, and it's early for lunch so it's empty. I get a cappuccino. The owner comes to chat with us, I tell him how beautiful his place is. There's an outdoor terrace surrounded by a field of grass, and all around are mountains. It is one of the best views ever. I tell him we are going a little farther on our hike and then we will be back for lunch. We have already picked our lunch out from the blackboard menu: ravioli for George and polenta with sausage for me. We keep going, this is a fairly flat dirt road and there are a few people. It's lovely, pine woods, little patches of grass, and clumps of wildflowers, purple and yellow and white.

We go back to lunch, there are people now, it's lunch time. There is a grandmother with two kids playing cards, occupying a lunch table but not ordering lunch. They are waiting for the parents, and seem oblivious to the fact that they are expected to consume. We have our lunch, George loves his, mine is not so great, strangely, it's so rare in Italy that any food is not great. It's also huge, so I leave some. But I don't mention it.

The owner is addressed by the other diners as "*Maestro*," not an orchestra conductor but a *maestro di sci*, a ski instructor, a venerable a profession here. Ski instructor and restaurateur, an Alpine genius.

VALTOURNENCHE AND CERVINIA

This is a famous valley in our family because it's where my mother and her family lived at the end of World War II. It's a famous valley in general because it's crowned by the Cervino, the Italian name for the Matterhorn. The Cervino may be the most well-known mountain profile in the world, it's mostly known from its Swiss side appearance, with a slightly crooked point. From the Italian side it's flat topped, it's a little different looking, and still majestic.

Valtournenche is the name of the valley and the name of the old town lower in the valley. Cervinia is the resort, right under the Matterhorn. You can't see the mountain from Valtournenche, you can see it well from Cervinia, though in our case, it will turn out, not so much. The valley is steep, everything is on a steep incline. Unlike Sestriere, which is on top of the world, wide open, in this valley you feel very much in the valley. There are tall mountains on all sides, very close by, rising up right above your head. Even in Cervinia, at the tippy top of the valley, the mountains rise up steeply, you're down below. Though we will rise above, we will go higher.

Valtournenche is a cheerful little town with many flowers. It's at 1,500 meters, about 5,000 feet, pretty high altitude. We stop and head to the church, which we find via the steeple. There's a little square in front of the church, and to the side a short covered walkway that leads to the main road. In front of the church is a small fountain. There's also an obelisk memorial. And also, all around the square in front of the church, attached to the side of the buildings, are many plaques commemorating the mountain climbers. There is a huge tradition of mountain climbing here, with the guides as the heroes. Though interestingly, the mountain itself, the Cervino, is not visible from here, it's a mythical unseen presence.

Everyone here is called Bich, Pellissier and Carrel. Almost everyone. It's evident and poignant that a few families embody that tradition that goes back, officially at least, for over a century. I can imagine that unofficially, people were familiar with these mountains going back many more years. The official organization Societa' delle Guide del Cervino was founded in 1865, the year in which the summit of the mountain was reached for the first time. The achievement was by an Englishman, a man named Whymper, but the second ascent that same year was by a Bich and a Carrel. The mountain is 4,500 meters high, about 15,000 feet. There's a Punta Carrel, at 3,800 meters.

It strikes me that these families are attached to this mountain, generation after generation. Their life and livelihood is here. There's a Bich and a Carrel in the current Guide del Cervino. This is so different from my own family, where each generation does something completely different from the prior one, and I wonder often what George will do. I expect him to do something different, something I can't predict right now, and I wonder how I can help him get there. Maybe I shouldn't help him, I shouldn't influence him, for fear of bringing him to the wrong career, not the one he should have pursued.

I am looking for a specific plaque, one that my aunt told me about. When they lived up here, she had a friend, a boy her age, not an admirer, she points out. He was a promising guide himself, his name was Camillo Carrel. Shortly after the war he fell while climbing, and died. It was a sad story when I heard her tell it, and it is more stirring now, thinking about it in the midst of this tradition and of all these Carrels commemorated on these plaques. I can see what a big deal climbing is here, how it's what this whole place is about, and I can imagine what a tragedy Camillo's death would have been—he was young and a promising guide both.

My aunt told me the plaque was near the walkway to the road, I look all over for it, I call her too and we talk about it, but I can't find it. I'm very disappointed.

This boy shared school books with my aunt, everything was makeshift then. My aunt, who was notoriously not studious, had to take her high school graduation exams. She and my grandmother went into the valley, for her to take the exams, this was a long distance, down to Ivrea, about 40 miles. My grandmother was known for being stubborn and she was going to get this done no matter what. My aunt tells me they walked and hitchhiked, "*Abbiamo fatto l'autostop.*" They were picked up by a military truck and they arrived safely.

She told me about it, she still remembers it. "I knew the material for the Italian exam, I had studied Italian." These were oral exams, in front of a panel of teachers. "But I knew nothing about physics, I hadn't studied it and I didn't know anything. When I got in front of the examiners, I told them my story. And they didn't ask me a single question." And she passed.

We walk into the bar on the church square, it's called Café des Guides. Of course. I get the usual cappuccino and George gets a Coke. As we stand there drinking our treats, a tall thin man walks in holding some paperwork in his hands. He addresses the man and the woman who are working the bar, he says that his is a *funzionario per la pubblicita'*, an advertising officer, he is in charge of collecting a fee for the bar's advertising. He is wearing very tight lime green pants and a turquoise polo shirt. This looks to me like the biggest scam on the planet, or certainly the biggest one in the valley on this nice August day. The workers are none too pleased to deal with him either. They do a little dance. He tells them that big brand publicity is paid by the big brands, but any local publicity, namely the little sign that tries to entice tourists to their little corner of the square, is taxable. They say they will take down the sign then. He says the fee is 20 euros. They seem to think that's not so bad. They are still dancing their little dance when we leave.

There's a tourist office, and we go in to ask about getting to Cheneil. This is a famous hike that my mother, my aunt, and Arianna did regularly and quickly. Cheneil consists of a few stone huts, there is no road. There is a hotel, called Panorama al Bich. We just missed the gondola, there's a gondola now. So we get directions to walk there, and we embark on the walk, which takes us through the back streets of the town. These so called streets are in fact narrow walkways that wind around the houses. They're very picturesque. The houses are alpine in style, made of stone and wood, with stone roofs, and huge flower boxes. We are walking uphill, and it's a nice walk, but I see that we are not going to be able to make this hike, it's too steep, too far, it will take too long. It's 2.5 kilometers, about 1.5 miles, and 500 meters up, about 1500 feet.

I feel that I will regret this because I don't know that I will ever be back here, and Cheneil is such a romantic place in my family history, but I don't think we can do this, not in our fast travel way. We are still planning to go up to Cervinia, and all in one day. So we turn back.

I did enjoy seeing the back walkways of Valtournenche. People live here, they've lived here for many years, in this mountain valley, under the tall peaks. My mother and my aunt lived here, in this place.

I had not asked my aunt ahead of time where exactly they lived, and it doesn't occur to me to ask her over the phone. It will turn out that they lived right across the road from the church, in what's now a hotel, Albergo Grandes Murailles, named after the surrounding peaks. I take a picture of the hotel unknowing of the significance, I take a picture of it because it's pretty.

I want to get a souvenir of Valtournenche, something for my mother and my aunt, that they can hang on to. We walk into a shop and I buy two oven mitts, a red one and a white one, embroidered with *stelle alpine*, edelweiss, one for each of them, so they each have a piece of Valtournenche, and they each have a piece of their joint history. They will both like the gift.

We pick up our drive again, going farther up the valley, we stop at the Lago Blu. This is supposed to be a pretty lake, with a bright reflection in it of the sky and the Cervino. It is however a bit overcast and there is a little cloud hanging on the mountain, so the lake is a dull dark green. George is hung up on this, "Why do they call it Blue Lake? It should be called Green Lake." He says this multiple times. On the flip side, in spite of the fact that the lake is a big nothing today, there are many people around it, so not only is it not that great, but it's also overcrowded. Time to go. We keep going up the road, to Cervinia.

And we soon get there, we get to Cervinia. We are now directly under the Cervino, and there is a little cloud hanging still on the mountain. It's right there, and we came all this way to see it, and we can't see it. We will be here all afternoon, and the cloud will be there all afternoon. We won't see the mountain with its iconic shaped top.

We walk up the main street in Cervinia. The buildings are bigger than in Valtournenche, but still very characteristic of the Alpine tradition, with lots of wood and stone and lots of flowers. Very pretty. I ask a woman sitting on a bench where the gondolas are that go up higher, and she points me in the right direction. We don't go right away though, first we need to find a place to eat.

We go in a crepe restaurant, the specialty is crepes, filled with all different kinds of fillers, both sweet and the opposite of sweet which is "savoury." Savoury crepes are filled with the likes of gorgonzola and walnuts, or eggplant and peppers, or tuna and artichokes. George selects a Nutella filled crepe, which he enjoys immensely. This is truly a feel good food, a meal of basically Nutella, how great is that!

We head for the gondolas, in a large building. In the winter, with all the skiers, it must be crowded. Right now it's cavernous and fairly deserted. I inquire at the ticket booth, I want to know that it entails, what we can do. She says there are three separate gondolas to get to the top, the price is fairly high, but we came all the way here, I want to go up. I wonder if there's enough time because it's already two o'clock, and she says yes, we have time to go up, hang out, and still catch the last gondola back. The last thing I wonder about is the visibility. Will we go all the way and and find out we are enshrouded in clouds. She shows me a web cam on her computer, there is visibility. It's truly just the Cervino itself that is in the clouds.

So we buy out tickets and we go. The first gondola is a small four-person cabin, though it's just the two of us inside. It runs continuously, there's a cabin every few meters. It goes up to a place called Plan Maison. From there we take a similar gondola to a place called Cime Bianche. From there we take a large single gondola. There's one going up, and one coming down, they cross in the middle. Each one holds 140 passengers according to the warning. It's just me and George and three men proudly wearing fleeces embroidered with the words Funivie del Cervino. I'm guessing it's a good job. This last gondola goes to the top, to Plateau Rosa, which is right on the Italian-Swiss border. I take a picture of George in front of the border sign, and he's smiling. The entire trip up took about 40 minutes and elevated us 1,500 meters, about 5,000 feet—in a very short horizontal distance. We will notice on the way down how steeply the gondolas rise and descend.

We get out and it's exciting, we are up so high, it's really cold up here! We are at 3,500 meters, about 11,000 feet. We look all around us and there are glaciers everywhere. This spot is famous for summer skiing, my sister and I did that when we were little one summer, we skied up here on the glaciers. Kind of an amazing thing to have done, of which I don't recall very much. It's also a spot for mountain climbing. And evidently for meditating. Up here in the cold there are skiers, mostly on their way down at this late time of day, fully geared up in ski clothing, there are the mountain climbers, fully geared up in mountain climbing duds, with crampons under their shoes, and then there's us, wearing one light sweater each and comfortable shoes, and a bunch of people sitting cross-legged on the ground, also inadequately clothed.

There's a small museum, we go inside to warm up. There's a big thermometer on the wall and the indoor temperature is 14 degrees Celsius, 57 Fahrenheit. We then head to the Rifugio Guide del

Cervino, a small restaurant. On the way there we step on the glaciers and slip slide around, next to people who are crampon soled. It's funny to be stupid sometimes. Inside we get pizza and hot chocolate. All the décor in the small restaurant is about mountain climbing, again the tradition and a big part of the economy I'm sure.

We head back to the gondola for the trip down the mountain. This is one the last gondolas of the day, and it's pretty crowded, mostly with the meditators. Going down, it's a little scary. Although the cabin moves slowly, it's dropping dramatically, we can't see the cabin in front of us, it's already below us, and it feels like we're going off the edge of the Earth. All in all, a fantastic place, otherworldly.

ZUCCARELLO AND ALBENGA

We drive by Zuccarello, unknowing. I've never heard of it. We're in a Ligurian valley, the usually curvy road in a steep wooded hillside, kind of like the road to Sassello, but this one is farther west. There's a place to leave the car, right along the road, so we do. We stop and leave the car. As it happens so often, our fate is determined by the availability of parking.

We enter the town, this unknown town. I have no expectations at all, and I find that it's lovely beyond lovely. The main street, curvy and narrow, without cars, is lined on both sides by porticos—for the entire length of it. Unlike the regularly patterned porticos built more recently, these are all different. Some are held up with stone columns, some with white stucco columns, some columns are round, some start out bigger and taper off as they go up. It's a fantastic place. And I had never heard of it! It makes me wonder how many other wonderful places exist that I don't know about.

There are a few other streets off this main street, but short ones. We go down one and arrive at the medieval arched bridge over a tiny river. There's a stone basin where the women once washed the family's clothes.

It's as usual an odd hour, around one o'clock, so no one is around. I can't tell if this place is always so quiet or not. I'm not sure what kind of place this is. Who lives here? I would like to live here, I think. I'm sure George would not consider the prospect even a little bit. He would think, it's not New Jersey. Which it's not.

There are no shops really, which is unusual for any Italian town. There's a small barely equipped bar. There's a restaurant with a sign saying it's closed because the owners had a baby.

We walk the whole street to the other end and back. What a lovely place.

We leave and head down to the coast, to Albenga. It's not far but it's not the prettiest of drives, there are various commercial buildings. I'm a little disappointed in that. Zuccarello is really a place unto itself, but its surroundings are not as magical. I continue to think about it. I would like to live here, it would be like living in a dream.

In Albenga we find the old town, with the usual tiny streets. We see a boy carrying a big bouquet of sunflowers. He is accompanied by a dog. A young man admires the flowers and tells the boy that he had once brought sunflowers to someone who was ill. The boy doesn't respond so we never find out who they were for.

Albenga has towers and it boasts a cultural life. This is a happening place.

We sit outdoors at a café to get some ice cream. It's now past two o'clock and we have not had lunch. The café' is called Carpe Diem. I think to myself that it's a sign, a sign about Zuccarello, I should seize the day and move there.

I go inside to get something to drink because we are thirsty, I get an *aranciata* S. Pellegrino. It has pulp sediment at the bottom so I shake it—lightly—and when I open it, it fizzes out all over the floor. It kind of breaks the day seizing moment: the people of Albenga now know that I am an idiot.

NOLI AND GROTTE DI BORGIO VEREZZI

Everyone knows that there are four Repubbliche Marinare, the maritime republics of the late Middle Ages, independent city states that traded all over the Mediterranean: they are Venice, Amalfi, Pisa and Genova. It turns out that Noli was a fifth one. The only way to know this is to go to Noli, where this information, which is guarded in secrecy from the outside world, is available here everywhere. This is a tiny town east of Savona, on the Mediterranean, that was an independent sovereign country and a maritime republic for a whopping 600 years, from 1193 to 1797.

It has walls and churches and a comfortable portico and the requisite ice cream store. Very nice indeed.

My cousin had suggested a visit to a prehistoric site. "After the tunnel," he said, "turn right." He has a good track record of steering us well, so I follow the instructions. Only there are multiple tunnels, none followed closely by a right turn, so I end up instead at an underground cave site. There are tours on the hour, our tour is made up of, in addition to us, an English family, another non-Italian family, an Italian family, and an older man who makes lame jokes. The tour guide is a young woman who explains everything in Italian and English both, and I think she knows more languages. As always, languages are very important in this tourist economy.

The caves are lovely, with many different formations, many of which are named based on their appearance. There are lakes inside, the formations are created by water, it's all about the water. The guide turns off the light so we can experience absolute darkness. The older man says, "Hey, no grabbing."

MADONNA DELLA GUARDIA

We had attempted an ascent a few years ago. We had had to abort though, because of tears. George cried beyond my endurance, and we had turned back.

Yet we always saw the little church at the top of the hill. At night too, all lit up, atop the dark hill, a little light in the middle of the sky almost.

I happened to see on a flyer posted outside another church that August 29th is the feast day at the little church, the feast of the Madonna della Guardia. There would be refreshments and *focaccette*, and a mass. So I decide we are going up to it on the feast day.

We leave the house relatively early, stop in town for a cappuccino and a *brioche*, and then drive up to where the trail begins. The trail is a rocky dirt road, there's a sign indicating it's 3 kilometers to the top, 2 miles. Which sounds harmless enough, but we know it's a grueling 2 miles, from our prior attempt. It's nine o'clock in the morning, pretty early, but already hot.

George almost immediately informs me, "I'm not having fun." He will repeat that refrain the whole way up. But he doesn't cry, so we keep going. It's hot and it's steep, but we keep going, with the occasional rest.

A man we had seen farther down on the road catches up to us while we're seated and resting. He's from here but he has never been up to the little church before.

We also encounter people descending already. I ask one about the road ahead. Is it tough? "It depends," is the reply. What does that mean? Later I realize they're underestimating me. It depends how tough I am. Ha! I will show them. Wait, who am I showing? A stranger? Or more likely myself.

One lady coming down tells me, "You have to go up early, like I did." Well thank you very much. Perhaps you could have told me that yesterday. Or you could have kept it to yourself. Your little triumphalism. Why does one feel the need to show up a complete stranger?

Up to this point, we have not been able to see the little church at all, we are below it and a valley over. One man tells us, "There's a rocky stretch and then you can see the church. Then it's easy." Once you see your destination, and that destination is inspiring or at least appealing, then it's easy. It's analogous to moving through life, and the man's statement turns out to be true, as it would be true in life. The church is still far, far and up, but we can see it, and because it's the feast day there's a string of little flags strung across a bit of sky and visible from where we are. It's festive.

Finally we get there, we get there. It only took an hour, not really that long, but it feels like a big accomplishment.

There are maybe twenty or thirty other people there, the big turnout for the feast day. They are locals, many of them are speaking in dialect, which is not just an inflection or word choice, it's a whole separate language. I understand it generally because my grandmother, although she spoke Italian too, preferred the dialect and used it often. It's a special language that's dying out with the younger generations.

The main entrance to the church faces the sea, not the road on which people arrive. It looks out to sea—out and below. Savona is to the right, Genova to the left. The church is cute inside, it's small, and there are flowers. There are a number of *ex voto*, most about accidents at sea. One concerns an accident on scaffolds: the picture shows a broken scaffold and a person in mid-fall.

We exit the church and make our way to the refreshment stand. We buy water and two salame sandwiches.

There's a mass starting soon. The bells peal over and over.

I tell George, "There's a mass starting soon."

"A mass what?" he asks. He goes to the Methodist church, he doesn't know what a mass is.

We don't stay for the mass, we are not the devout, we came on a personal journey, we accomplished something, this ascent, that we had failed at previously. Maybe on her feast day, the Madonna helped us up.

SHOES

My aunt has had a bad knee the entire time we've been here. She really can't walk much, even around the house. She hit her knee walking in her bedroom in the dark.

She's sitting on her bed in the morning, in her nightgown, and we are talking about her knee, and the conversation moves to her shoes. She wears little dainty shoes always, flat heeled but dainty—no support. I talk about my shoes, I just bought them for this trip, they are hiking shoes, basically sneakers, with a big running shoe sole, but light brown. I tell her to try them on, she says no, she has big feet. I tell her I have big feet too, and I demonstrate by wearing her dainty shoes and showing her that my big toe goes all the way to the end.

She thinks about it, then she agrees to try on one shoe, to be polite I think. Then she puts on the other shoe, and gets up and walks up and down the room.

"They are comfortable," she admits. And she accepts the shoes. I'm here for two weeks, eating her food, and in exchange I give her a pair of used shoes. Stinky too.

When she comes downstairs she's wearing a skirt instead of the usual pants, and it's because she didn't take the shoes off to get dressed. She will tell my mother ongoing that my shoes are so comfortable. I think she really likes them.

Shakespeare says that there are more things in heaven and earth than Horatio can imagine, but I don't believe that, at least as it pertains to earth. There are only so many things, and variations of the same things, that reappear over and over again, in different forms, at different times, only so many things. And only so many shoes.

SASSELLO

Back to Sassello, we go to a small churchyard a little above the town, there's no one here. There's a memorial along a wall of all the war dead from Sassello, across all wars. It starts with *Altre Guerre*, all other wars, then it moves to World War I and then World War II, separated by location, Russian front, Greek front, then those fallen for liberty, which I take to mean the partisans, and then non-military victims. Many of the fallen have the same last names, they are from the same families. I wonder about these men from Sassello, fighting in Russia. I really can't imagine what it must have been like for them. There's a small glass vial at the bottom of the memorial, marked *Sabbia del Don*. Someone brought back a little bit of sand from the River Don.

We stop by Bar Gina for our ice cream, and Gina is not there. There's a little museum across the street, a well done museum, the highlight of which for me are the ceilings of the rooms, all decorated with painted flowers. I ask the young woman who works there about Gina, and she tells me she must be taking her nap. What a relief.

We go up to San Giovanni, the pretty church a little above the town. This is the prettiest church in the world, I think. There's a wedding today, and the Just Married car is a white VW bug.

I tell George that I think this might be the last time ever that we come here, and he says, "Don't be sad."

THE LAST CHAPTER

The saying goes: the more things change, the more they stay the same. For me it's been the opposite: the more things stay the same, the more they change.

When I first came back to visit, I thought everything was the same, and much of it was. I could share with George exactly the way it was, "This is where my sister and I used to sit, this is the ice cream we liked, this is where my grandparents lived." Over the years that I visited though, some of my most dear people that I visited passed away, and while the buildings still look the same, it's just not the same. George grew too, and he never really took to Italy as I had thought he would.

The past is wonderful, but by definition it's just not there anymore. I am what I've become, I am now the outcome of everything I've done over the years, and the future will continue to be new, the further extension of everything I've done and everything I will still do.

Paul Theroux says, about travel: "If one is loved and feels free and has gotten to know the world somewhat, travel is simpler and happier."

The same applies to life: If one is loved and feels free and has gotten to know the world somewhat, life is simpler and happier.

That's very much how I feel right now. I know I'm loved, I have strong connections that mean a lot to me, and they love me back. I know I'm free, I come and go, I've had the freedom to stumble upon my life, an unusual life, and I have the independence to choose what comes next. I have gotten to know the world somewhat. The act of traveling itself, even in fairly familiar territory, clearly shows how big and varied the world is, and how spectacular and novel and uncertain it is. It lets me visualize many possibilities: if all these people live all these different lives, there really is a lot of life to choose from.

And for all his complaints, I believe the travel does the same for George too. I believe that he will be a fuller person from our trips. For him too, I hope that the past will be wonderful, and he will be what he will become, out of all his experiences, and be always a new and better person.

ABOUT THE AUTHOR

Olga Vannucci was born in Italy, lived in Brazil,
and came to the United States to attend Brown University.
She lives in rural New Jersey with her beloved son, George.

www.ingramcontent.com/pod-product-compliance
Lightning Source LLC
Chambersburg PA
CBHW022356040426
42450CB00005B/206